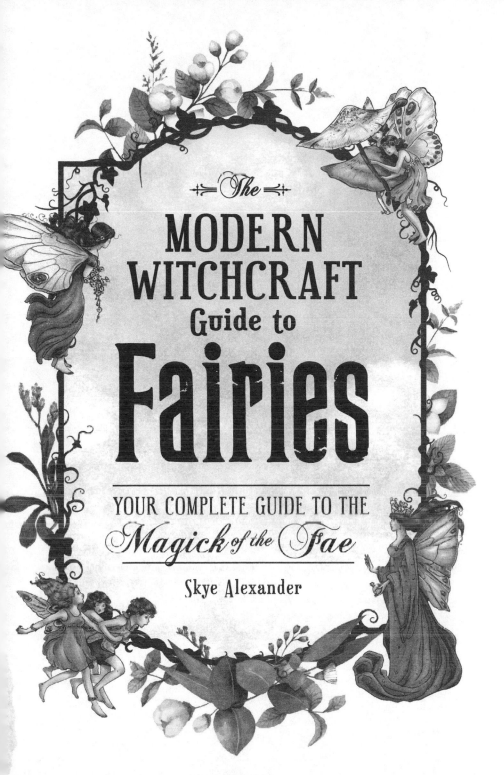

The

MODERN WITCHCRAFT

Guide to

Fairies

YOUR COMPLETE GUIDE TO THE

Magick of the Fae

Skye Alexander

Adams Media

New York London Toronto Sydney New Delhi

Adams Media
An Imprint of Simon & Schuster, Inc.
100 Technology Center Drive
Stoughton, Massachusetts 02072

First Adams Media hardcover
edition June 2021

ADAMS MEDIA and colophon are
trademarks of Simon & Schuster.

For information about special
discounts for bulk purchases, please
contact Simon & Schuster Special
Sales at 1-866-506-1949 or
business@simonandschuster.com.

The Simon & Schuster Speakers
Bureau can bring authors to your
live event. For more information or
to book an event contact the Simon
& Schuster Speakers Bureau at
1-866-248-3049 or visit our website
at www.simonspeakers.com.

Interior design by Priscilla Yuen
Interior images © 123RF/Denis
Barbulat, Elena Medvedeva,
elenamiv, laurent davoust, roystudio,
donatas1205; Getty Images/
bauhaus1000; Dover Publications

Manufactured in the United States
of America

1 2021

Library of Congress Cataloging-in-
Publication Data has been applied
for.

ISBN 978-1-5072-1591-3
ISBN 978-1-5072-1592-0 (ebook)

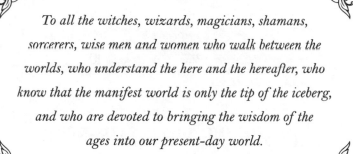

*To all the witches, wizards, magicians, shamans,
sorcerers, wise men and women who walk between the
worlds, who understand the here and the hereafter, who
know that the manifest world is only the tip of the iceberg,
and who are devoted to bringing the wisdom of the
ages into our present-day world.*

Acknowledgments

Once again, I am grateful for the vision, guidance, and wisdom of the wonderful Adams Media staff, whom I've had the pleasure to work with for many years. I especially wish to thank my team of editors, Peter Archer, Eileen Mullan, and Rebecca Tarr Thomas, for making this book possible. Many thanks, too, to all my readers, whose interest in my work and the Modern Witchcraft series in particular enables me to continue sharing the insights I've gained with other witches and magick practitioners around the world. As the Buddha is quoted as saying, "Thousands of candles can be lit from a single candle and the life of the candle will not be shortened. Happiness never decreases from being shared." May we continue to burn brightly, lighting each other's flames to dispel the darkness.

CONTENTS

PART TWO
SPELLS, RITUALS, AND PRACTICES FOR WORKING WITH FAIRIES THROUGHOUT THE YEAR 87

Chapter 7 WORKING WITH FAIRIES FOR PROSPERITY AND ABUNDANCE 113

Chapter 8 WORKING WITH FAIRIES FOR SAFETY AND PROTECTION 135

Chapter 9 WORKING WITH FAIRIES FOR HEALTH AND HEALING 161

Chapter 10 WORKING WITH FAIRIES FOR PERSONAL AND PROFESSIONAL SUCCESS 183

Chapter 11 WORKING WITH FAIRIES FOR PERSONAL AND SPIRITUAL GROWTH 207

Introduction

When you hear the word "fairy," what image comes to mind? A miniature girl with gossamer wings and a sparkly dress, à la Disney's version of Tinker Bell? A benevolent creature who flits about sprinkling fairy dust everywhere, waving her wand to make children's wishes come true? If so, you're in for a surprise.

Like unicorns and mermaids, these magickal entities have been denatured by pop culture, robbed of their mystique and majesty. The fairies of old were nothing like the sugar-coated cartoon characters we envision today. They were powerful beings of a semidivine nature, who may have descended from the gods and goddesses. According to some tales, they served as the prototypes from which the human race evolved. They possessed amazing, supernatural powers—they could fly, make themselves invisible, shapeshift into humans, animals, plants, or stones, and they lived forever. Some aided human beings, but many were mischievous or even malevolent.

The English word "fairy" may have come from the Latin *fatum*, meaning "fate," as did the French derivative *fée*, the Italian *fata*, and the Portuguese *fada*. According to some legends, fairies controlled human destiny. They showed up at a baby's birth to celebrate the new arrival, as the story of Sleeping Beauty tells us, and to determine the child's future—which depended on how the parents treated the fairies.

Fairies could provide healing and protection from harm, but they could also inflict illness, shipwreck sailors, and cause soldiers to falter on the battlefield. They could bring riches, but they might also blight crops, destroy livestock, and steal children. As in the human world, the fairy realm has its good guys and its bad actors. Wiccans who follow the Wiccan Rede will not use their connections to fairies for harm; instead, they'll finds ways to harness their powers for the good of all.

How to Use This Book

In this book, you'll learn how to reconnect, through Wiccan practices, with these magickal beings who fascinated and frightened our ancestors. You'll gain insight into their characteristics and behavior. You'll find out where and how they live. You'll discover ways to attract and interact safely with fairy helpers. In doing so, if the fairies are friendly, you can improve and enhance your Wiccan powers.

In Part One, I discuss the long-standing links between witches and fairies. Our ancestors believed witches and fairies shared numerous powers, including the ability to control the weather. According to some sources, the fairies taught witches their craft. I also talk about why the two groups can benefit from collaborating today and how working together can help not only us but the planet as well.

You'll meet some of the best-known fairy families and learn about various types of fairies with whom you may want to do magick—and some you should avoid. Like people, some fairies are better suited to certain kinds of spellwork than others. For instance, leprechauns are solitary old guys and wouldn't be much good at casting love spells—but they're skilled in money matters and can help you prosper financially. Nature fairies, who care for the plant world, could be great allies for green witches. I also share some of the things I've discovered about where to look for fairies and how to entice them to partner with you, because they're usually reluctant to deal with humans. Additionally, you'll learn how to avoid offending the fae, who can be dangerous enemies if you get on the wrong side of them.

Part Two is an open grimoire of spells, rituals, and other activities you can do with the fairies. Each chapter focuses on a particular area of life, such as love, prosperity, protection, healing, and so on. I've included a chapter of magickal activities to engage in with the fae on each of the eight sabbats too. Some of these practices will be familiar to you—if you've been following the witch's way for any length of time, you've surely used candles, herbs, and gemstones in your work. Performing them with fairies, however, will add a new dimension. Other techniques, such as shapeshifting and shamanic journeying, may be new to you—especially if you're visiting fairyland for the first time. At the beginning of each chapter, I suggest certain types of fairies that I think might be the most willing and able to assist you in your spellcraft.

At the end of the book is an Appendix that I hope you'll find helpful and easy to use. This isn't intended to be all-inclusive—it's not an encyclopedia—but it can serve as quick reference guide when you're deciding what to factor into your spells.

Working with the fae and integrating them into your Wiccan practices can be a rewarding experience that brings added depth and breadth to your magickal endeavors. It will enrich your self-knowledge and power. Allying yourself with fairies will also increase your appreciation for the natural world, other worlds, and for all beings who inhabit the physical and nonphysical realms. If you feel drawn to follow this path, you'll be rewarded on your journey. But proceed with care.

Blessed Be.

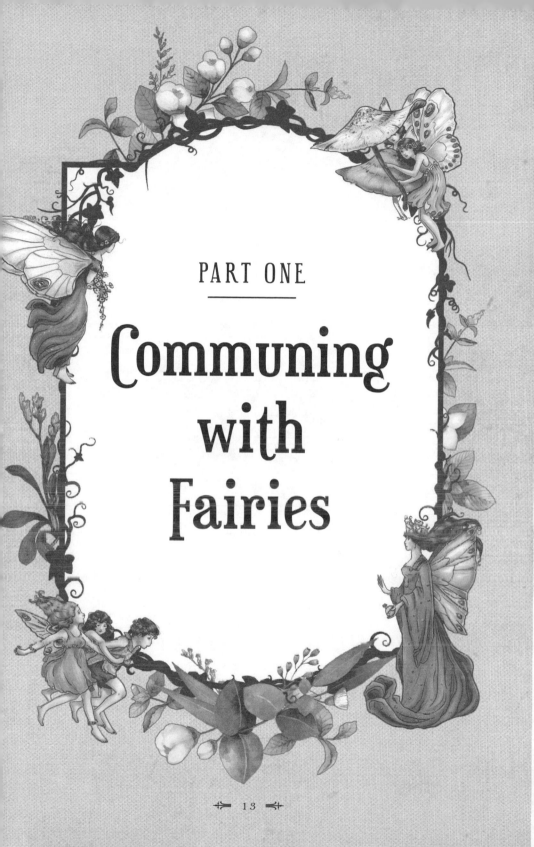

PART ONE

Communing
with
Fairies

Chapter 1

WITCHCRAFT AND FAIRIES

From distant ages past, magickal beings of all shapes and sizes populated the earth and the mystical realms beyond. Some were giants, some the size of humans, and others tiny enough to ride on the backs of birds. They lived in lakes, trees, and underground barrows. Some had wings and could fly through the sky. "They spring from fountains and from sacred groves / And holy streams that flow into Rübezabl the sea," wrote the Greek poet Homer, nearly three thousand years ago.

Many fairies eschewed contact with human beings, but some interacted with people and even mated with them, as folklore and eyewitness accounts from around the world attest. The people the fairies often chose to meet with were witches, in earlier times as well as today. That's because witches are accustomed to working with the spirit world. Many of us honor and commune with goddesses and gods. We nurture relationships with nonphysical entities such as guides, guardians, angels, and spirit animals. Through our magickal practices, we've honed our senses to become aware of things that most people never see. Simply put, we're more likely to connect with fairies because we believe they exist.

In this chapter, we'll examine the background of fairies and how they fit into the world of Wicca. It's important to note that fairies, by their own choice, stand well apart from the world of humans, even those such as practitioners of Wicca, who have an affinity for them.

RESPECT NATURE

Another reason fairies make themselves known to witches is because we respect nature. Legends from numerous cultures tell us that both fairies and witches have the power to influence the weather. Many fairies are spirits who serve as protectors of the natural world. Some accounts say these spirits actually animate plants and stones—they're the life force within all things in nature. So whenever you work with nature, whenever you do spells with herbs or crystals, you're working with the fairies too.

Tree Fairies

According to Greek mythology, every tree had a fairy in residence. When the tree died, the fairy departed. Legends from the Isles of Hesperides say fairies care for orchards of apple trees whose fruit brings immortality.

Both witches and fairies use plant magick for healing and myriad other purposes. You may already be familiar with brewing teas, dressing candles with essential oils, and making herbal potions and lotions. Through working with the fae you'll become even more skilled at bringing botanicals into your spellcraft. Part Two of this book includes a number of spells that draw upon the powers of flowers, herbs, and other plants, as well as fairy assistance. The Appendix lists herbs, gemstones, and other natural ingredients you may choose to use in your magickal practice.

Now let's look at some of the connections between witches and fairies, in the present day and in the past. As you'll see, ancient wise men and women may have received guidance from the fae for healing, divination, and many other time-honored skills that witches still engage in today. Legends and lore link the two species and even speak of mixed-blood beings. In this chapter, you'll also read examples of how fairies played a part in the notorious witchcraft trials in Britain, Ireland, and elsewhere during the Burning Times that raged across Europe from the fourteenth through the eighteenth centuries. And you'll learn about some of the powers fairies wield, as well as how witches and fairies can collaborate today for the benefit of all beings on our planet.

WHY FOCUS ON CELTIC FAIRIES?

Much—though by no means all—of the material in this book focuses on the fairies of Celtic lore, specifically those of the British Isles and Ireland. I've chosen this direction because the traditions and practices of many modern Wiccans, neopagans, and Western witches derive from the Old Religion of these countries. Celtic legends are richly imbued with tales of the fae and contain a colorful cast of characters. If you have Celtic blood flowing in your veins, as I do, you may already sense an affinity with the fairy world. Our myths and legends, our history, art, and music, are steeped in magick, a magick that reaches deep into the unseen worlds where spirits and mystical beings of all kinds—including fairies—abide.

However, you'll also find information here about many other kinds of fairies from around the world. These, too, are important to Wiccans. For thousands of years, people around the world have told stories of fairies: the German nixie, the Russian leshiye, the Persian peris. We find tales of fairies interacting with human beings—and particularly witches—on all continents.

> "The ancient Celts were various population groups living in several parts of Europe north of the Mediterranean region from the Late Bronze Age onwards....In antiquity writers did not describe tribes in ancient Britain and Ireland as Celts, although they have acquired that label in modern times and some Celtic languages or their derivatives are still spoken there, as a form of Celtic still is in the Brittany region of northern France. The religion of the Celts [was] led by a priesthood known as the Druids."
>
> MARK CARTWRIGHT, historian

FAIRY WITCHCRAFT

Common interests and objectives between witches and fairies have led to the development of what's known as Fairy Witchcraft. Based in age-old beliefs, mainly of Celtic derivation, this modern branch of the Craft of the Wise combines neopaganism with the Fairy Faith that has existed for centuries, especially in Ireland and Scotland. "Fairy Faith" refers both to the ancient folkloric tradition of the fae and the contemporary version that began in the 1970s. However, you needn't be of Celtic heritage to tread this path—you can be of any lineage, culture, or religion. Those who choose the way of Fairy Witchcraft partner with the fae for the good of both species and for Mother Earth as well.

Faery Wicca

There's even a branch of Wicca called Faery Wicca, founded by author Kisma Stepanich. This modern tradition draws upon Irish myths of the Tuatha dé Danann—deities who predate humankind—and emphasizes fairy lore in its practices. If you're interested in tarot, you may want to check out the *Faery Wicca Tarot* deck, illustrated by Renée Christine Yates.

Although you'll find many aspects of Fairy Witchcraft similar to those of other witchy paths—the eight sabbats in the Wheel of the Year, for example—it places more emphasis on journeywork into other realms of existence, the Otherworld in particular. (We'll talk more about the Otherworld later.) Engaging with the fae and doing magick with them, as you might expect, is an important part of this system.

Another area that's distinctive to Fairy Witchcraft is the deities it recognizes. Wiccans, for example, revere the Goddess as the primary divine power in the universe, and the God as her consort. They also honor various other goddesses and gods—my books *Find Your Goddess* and *Your Goddess Year* discuss many of these. Followers of Fairy Witchcraft additionally respect four main divinities known as the Lady of the Greenwood and the Lord of the Wildwood, who reign during the six months between Beltane and Samhain, and the Queen of the Wind and the Hunter, who preside over the other half of the year.

> "Fairy Witchcraft is a modern faith that offers a way for pagans to connect deeply to the Fairy Faith of old by seeking to revive some of the old traditional practices while looking to a neopagan religious framework. At heart it is a wild and experiential path that encourages the witch to learn how to safely reach out to the Otherworld and to take chances to create connections to Fairy which involve risk balanced with wisdom."
>
> **MORGAN DAIMLER,** *Fairycraft*

SPIRITS OF THE MOUNDS

According to some scholars, our reverence for and fascination with fairies may be rooted in the ancestor worship practiced in many ancient, indigenous cultures. Ancestor worship is common among people as diverse as the Chinese and the native tribes of North America, as well as the early Celts. Researchers base this supposition on the fact that Irish and Germanic folklore link the fairies known as the *sidhe* and the *alfar*, respectively, with burial mounds. The bones of tribal leaders and highly esteemed persons were interred in these mounds. Over time, folklore tells us, the mounds became homes to the spirits we now call fairies.

Mysterious Barrows

Throughout Europe, our ancestors constructed thousands of "barrows," underground chambers whose purposes still mystify us. Researchers theorize these mounds, such as the West Kennet Long Barrow in Wiltshire, England, which contemporary pagans consider a sacred site, may have served as places for ancestor worship, because archaeologists have discovered human remains in many of them. The oldest of these barrows are located in western France and date back more than twenty-five hundred years. They show up in Spain, the Netherlands, and Scandinavia as well as the British Isles and Ireland.

Another theory suggests that fairies descended from indigenous gods and goddesses, who were displaced when Christianity prevailed in Britain, Ireland, and elsewhere. Some stories described them as fallen angels. Christian beliefs also classified fairies as demons. People suspected of associating with fairies were frequently denounced as witches and persecuted.

Once powerful divinities, of whom the Irish Tuatha dé Danann are the best known, these demoted and denigrated spirits are said to have taken up residence in these magickal mounds, as well as in the woodlands, lakes, and caves of Europe. But despite the Church's attempts to supplant them, the fairies continued to keep the people in their thrall—and do to this day.

MORGAN LE FAY, THE MOST FAMOUS FAIRY WITCH OF ALL

One of the most intriguing and enigmatic characters in the Arthurian legends, Morgan le Fay has been depicted in various ways by various writers: as a powerful queen, a demon, an enchantress, a priestess, a sorcerer, a healer, a protector of the old ways. Possibly she evolved from the Irish goddess of war and destiny known as the Morrigan, who used magick as her weapon in battle. By many accounts, she's a witch and spellworker, who learned her craft from the wizard Merlin. She's also a fairy—her name, le Fay, proclaims her lineage—albeit only half (the other half is human). The captivating Morgan lived on the magickal Isle of Avalon inhabited by the fae, a realm beyond the veil, removed from the material world and hidden in mists.

Mari-Morgans

Arthurian scholars Lucy Allen Paton and Norris Lacy suggest Morgan's story may have originated in the folklore of Brittany. There, the term "mari-morgans" is used for a type of fairy otherwise known as a sprite.

England's Geoffrey of Monmouth first discussed the beguiling Morgan in the mid-twelfth century in his *Vita Merlini*. He described her as an otherworldly being and a healer. Later in that century, French author Chrétien de Troyes wrote that Morgan was King Arthur's half-sister and an astrologer. According to Sir Thomas Malory in his fifteenth-century version of the legends, *Le Morte d'Arthur*, Morgan was a supernatural being, a sorceress schooled in witchcraft.

More recently, Mark Twain cast her as a villain—a cunning human one—in *A Connecticut Yankee in King Arthur's Court*. In *The Mists of Avalon*, Marion Zimmer Bradley portrayed her as a pagan priestess defending the Old Religion during the rise of Christianity in Britain.

> "Morgan le Fay knew men's weaknesses and discounted their strengths. And she knew also that most improbable actions may be successful so long as they are undertaken boldly and without hesitation."
>
> **JOHN STEINBECK,** *The Acts of King Arthur and His Noble Knights*

Those who demonize Morgan may do so because she symbolizes feminine power and challenges the organized system of male domination that has existed for centuries. She's the quintessential "femme fatale," both beautiful and dangerous, a female who belongs to no man. Other detractors may object to her mixed blood, which gives her abilities beyond those of mere mortals and which excludes her from either race. Whoever Morgan le Fay was, or is, she remains one of the most engaging, complex, and timeless characters in English literature.

WITCHES AND FAIRIES IN THE BURNING TIMES

During the Medieval and Renaissance periods, fairies held a prominent place in folklore throughout much of Europe, and many people believed in the awesome powers of the fae. Witches were often said to gain their magickal abilities from the fairies. From the fourteenth through the eighteenth centuries, in what's known as the "Burning Times," tens of thousands of people—most of them women—were executed in Europe and the British Isles for the crime of witchcraft. In many instances, the so-called witches were also accused of being in league with fairies.

At one famous trial that took place in Palermo, Sicily, in 1588, a fisherman's wife charged with being a witch claimed to have cavorted with the King and Queen of Elves. She stated that she could leave her physical body whenever she wanted to dine with the fae, and that they promised her riches. Because faith in fairies was so strong at the time, her explanation convinced her accusers to release her. Instead of being condemned for associating with the devil, she was found guilty of having dreams of fairies.

In the last quarter of the sixteenth century, several Scottish women who were tried for witchcraft testified they'd learned their craft from the fae. Janet Boyman of Edinburgh said the "Good Neighbors" (a respectful term for fairies) had taught her the art of healing. Elizabeth Dunlop of Ayrshire described having learned to heal, divine the future, and locate lost items from the elf queen and fairies she called the "good wights." Allison Pearson of Fife professed to have gained her healing knowledge from green-garbed men and women who possessed superhuman powers. And in Edinburgh, Christian Lewinston told a court she'd learned witchcraft from her daughter, who'd been kidnapped and schooled by fairies.

In another well-known trial at Auldearn on the Moray Firth, Scotland, in 1662, Isobel Gowdie was accused of witchcraft. Gowdie testified that she met with Queen Elphame of the Fairies over a period of years, in Scotland's caves and hills. According to Gowdie, the fairy taught her to fly using a beanstalk, to shapeshift into animals, to blight crops, and to raise storms.

One historic Irish example is of herbalist "Biddy" Early (1798–1874), who was known for successfully using herbs to treat both humans and animals. Early claimed the fairies taught her plant medicine. She carried a mysterious bottle with her everywhere—supposedly it related fairy secrets to her. In 1865 she was accused of witchcraft, but her fellow townspeople wouldn't testify against her and she went free for lack of evidence.

Professor Ronald Hutton, author of *The Witch: A History of Fear, From Ancient Times to the Present*, points out that few people were executed as witches in Ireland, Wales, the Scottish Highlands, and the Hebrides (although nearly four thousand were put to death in other parts of Scotland during the witch trials). Hutton suggests this was because "in the case of Gaelic Scotland, the local spirits of land and water were regarded as being especially ferocious and dangerous, perhaps because of the formidable nature of the terrain, and the same exceptional fear was accorded to the local equivalent of elves and fairies, the *sithean*...for committing precisely those attacks upon humans and their animals and homes that were credited elsewhere to witches."

FAIRIES' MAGICKAL POWERS

Today, most people think fairies are cute, cuddly, lovable little creatures your child would like to have as friends. But that's not the case. Fairies embody good and evil, innocence and passion, playfulness and treachery. Some are bewitchingly beautiful; others are ugly enough to shatter mirrors.

Of course, they possess magickal powers—that's why they fascinate and frighten us. The problem is, you never know how they'll use those powers. If they like you, they may give you a pot of gold or make sure you have a safe journey. They can heal illnesses, boost your career, or protect you and your home. But they can also wreak havoc in your life or put a devastating spell on you. Remember what happened to Sleeping Beauty? The fae giveth and the fae taketh away.

> "Robert Kirk [Gaelic scholar and folklorist] believed the fairies to be the doubles or, as he called them, the 'co-walkers' of men, which accompanied them through life, and thought that this co-walker returned to Faerie when the person died."
>
> LEWIS SPENCE, *British Fairy Origins*

Although fairies have a wide range of magickal talents, some of the best known are:

- They can make themselves invisible.
- They can change shape to become animals, birds, trees—anything they choose.
- They live practically forever, and they don't get wrinkles or lose their prowess with the passage of time.
- They control the weather—they can paint rainbows in the sky or whip up ferocious storms just by snapping their fingers.
- They have amazing healing skills, but they've also been known to conjure plagues and pestilence.
- They can divine the future and in some cases manipulate it.

Obviously, we humans want to garner the fairies' goodies while avoiding their wrath. The problem is, the fae don't abide by the same rules we do, and they're notoriously capricious. That's not to say they don't have a code of ethics—they do, and it's a strict one. It's just not what we're accustomed to. So, in order to gain their assistance and encourage them to share their magick secrets with us, we need to understand them better.

NATURE FAIRIES

Let's talk some more about the fairies who guard and guide the natural world. Sometimes called nature spirits, they nurture, protect, and direct plant and animal life on Mother Earth. Some sources say they even implant ancient wisdom into crystals and gemstones, enabling the stones to work healing magick (more about this later).

Historically, nature fairies inhabited the wild places on our planet—and they still do. These spirits tend to be reclusive and solitary. They live in underground barrows, mountain caves, or beneath sacred lakes. Germany's nixies dwell in secret regions below streams and waterfalls. Trees, too, offer habitats for fairies, and legends say that no old tree is devoid of fairy occupants. The Welsh Tylwyth Teg, for instance, live deep in the woods on isolated islands off the coast of Wales. In Russia's forests, known as the *taiga*, woodland fairies called the leshiye reign supreme among the august trees.

"For all the hillside was haunted
By the faery folk come again
And down in the heart-light enchanted
Were opal-coloured men."

GEORGE WILLIAM RUSSELL,
"The Dream of the Children," *The Irish Theosophist*

Now that human beings have intruded into their domain by building skyscrapers, superhighways, and factories where forests and fields once flourished, the fairies have retreated to remote areas that remain relatively unscathed. According to some sources, the fae have gone underground, literally. But even in the world's major metropolises, we can still find nature spirits in public places. New York's Central Park, England's Kew Gardens, and Japan's Kyoto Botanical Garden couldn't survive without them.

"It is my belief that we need to reconnect with faerie, plant, animal, and mineral beings in mutual respect in order to restore harmony and balance to our minds and bodies, as well as healing to the many areas of our planet that we have damaged."

BERNADETTE WULF, author

Although nature fairies usually steer clear of humans, they'll work with earth-honoring witches and other ecologically minded people for the benefit of all. If you're a green witch, you probably already have the fairies' stamp of approval. If your magickal practice involves botanical witchery or herbal healing, it's especially important that you connect with these spirits and earn their favor.

How can you please the nature fairies?

- Plant a garden (don't use chemical fertilizers or pesticides).
- Pick up trash on a beach, in a park, or in your neighborhood.
- Use recycled products and recycle your waste.
- Leave food for wild birds and animals.
- Buy organic produce.
- Donate to organizations that protect the environment.
- Help out at an animal rescue shelter.

In our modern era, when air and water pollution, oil spills, deforestation, human-induced climate change, and other forms of environmental destruction threaten our planet, nature fairies have their hands full trying to cope. You can help, and your efforts will be rewarded by the fae.

FAIRIES OF FATE

Another group of fairies deals with destiny and the fate of humankind. The legends of many countries feature supernatural beings, sometimes referred to as "birth spirits," who control the fate of individual people and entire nations. The Norse spoke of three spirits known as the norns, who personified the past, present, and future. This trio charted the course of each person's life. In Greek mythology, three sisters called the Moirae determined destiny. Clotho, the eldest, spun the thread used to stitch together human life. Lachesis, the middle sister, measured the thread and decided how long a person would live. The youngest, Atropos, cut the thread at the moment of death.

The Portuguese refer to the fairies of fate as the *fada*. In Serbia, they're called the *oosood*, and in Albania the *fatit*. The ancient Egyptians believed seven sisters known as the Seven Hathors attended births, where they played tambourines and foretold the babies' futures.

According to Celtic folklore, a Fairy Queen and King not only governed their fairy subjects; they involved themselves in the fate of human beings as well. In his delightful play about the fae, *A Midsummer*

Night's Dream, Shakespeare named this queen and king Titania and Oberon. Elsewhere, the queen is called Mab. Irish legends tell us Una was the last queen of the *daoine sidhe,* the fairy descendants of the Tuatha dé Danann (more about them in the next chapter). Queen Elphame is her counterpart in the lore of Northern England and the Scottish Lowlands.

Guiding destiny is a big responsibility and a heady power. Therefore, the fairies of fate must be treated with the utmost respect by witches and others. Some traditions say parents should throw a feast for the fairies who attend a birth, just to make sure their children get a good chance in life. And if you happen to live in Brittany, be sure to include champagne!

FAIRY TALES AS MORALITY LESSONS

Most of us learned about the fae through fairy tales read to us as children. But although these fanciful stories may entertain, they had another purpose originally. In earlier times—especially during the Victorian era—fairy tales served as morality lessons for children. Through the vehicle of story, youngsters learned about good and evil; rewards and punishment; as well as the norms, rules, and expectations of the cultures in which they lived. If they misbehaved or rebelled against conventions, they could be sure the fairies would reprimand them. As James Whitcomb Riley's 1885 poem "Little Orphant Annie"—originally titled "The Elf Child"—warned disobedient kids, "the gobble-uns'll git you ef you don't watch out!"

A Moral Education

Austrian psychiatrist Bruno Bettelheim, in his book *The Uses of Enchantment: The Meaning and Importance of Fairy Tales,* wrote that children need "a moral education...[that teaches] not through abstract ethical concepts but through that which seems tangibly right and therefore meaningful....The child finds this kind of meaning through fairy tales."

Fairy tales, like the fables and epics that predated them, held meanings intended for adults too. During the Medieval and Renaissance periods, when belief in fairies was strong throughout much of Europe, men and women who committed crimes were threatened with fairy retribution—even if they escaped the law. Those who acted virtuously, however, could win favors from the fae. Cinderella became a princess (thanks to her fairy godmother's magickal assistance), whereas her wicked sisters lost out. The hardworking little pig's house withstood the big bad wolf's attack, but the homes of the two lazy, slipshod pigs got blown down.

Older fairy tales tended to be darker and more gruesome than the ones we enjoy now. Sometimes things didn't turn out well even for the good guys, if the fairy tale was intended to convey a moral message. In Hans Christian Andersen's original story "The Little Mermaid," for example, the heroine has her tongue cut out, sacrifices her lovely voice, and suffers terrible pain each time she takes a step on the legs for which she traded her fishy tail—and in the end, her beloved prince marries another woman. The story warned women to accept their lot in life and stay in their place, rather than aspiring for something greater.

Today's fairy tales, and the revised editions of classic tales, have been cleaned up for modern audiences. We prefer happy endings these days. Still, contemporary fairy tales and their counterparts contain the same basic elements they always have: hero/ines and villains, the struggle between good and evil, and the journey from innocence to wisdom (a journey the tarot depicts in its Major Arcana cards). And they still serve as moral compasses to guide, instruct, and inspire us. Today many Wiccans are rediscovering fairy tales as a valuable teaching tool and moral guide.

WHY WITCHES AND FAIRIES CAN BENEFIT FROM COOPERATING TODAY

Are fairies more or less likely to collaborate with humans today than in centuries past? It's hard to say. Legends tell us that many fairies have disappeared from the earth realm and no longer want to have anything to do with mortals. However, among witches and neopagans the interest in fairy magick appears to be growing—and our interest may draw them back to our world.

Frankly, we need each other. The fairies, whose job it is to take care of the earth and her inhabitants, need human beings to get onboard in order to save the planet. We've done untold damage already. Now it's time to take stock of the situation and make the necessary changes that will enable all forms of life to flourish here once again. Therefore, the nature fairies have a vested interest in partnering with us to speed up the process. Perhaps the fierce storms, earthquakes, and other natural catastrophes we've experienced in recent decades are a wake-up call from the fae, who legends say control the weather, and we should pay attention.

> "The sacredness of the land and planet is a major concern for us today.... If we are concerned about the land, the planet, the environment, we will have to change ourselves; we are the land, the environment...we are not separate from one another."
>
> R.J. STEWART, *Earth Light*

We humans need the fairies to teach us how to expand our imagination and intuition. Albert Einstein once stated that "imagination is more important than knowledge. For knowledge is limited to all we now know and understand, while imagination embraces the entire world, and all there ever will be to know and understand." According to some sources, fairies constantly slip insights to us, and many of our greatest inspirations have come from them.

As we advance technologically and materially, we're losing our connection not only to the natural world but also to the world of spirit. Fairies can help us reawaken our awareness of other levels of existence and dimensions of consciousness. Additionally, they can teach us to appreciate other species—physical and nonphysical. Doing so will enable us to gain wisdom and receive guidance from spirits, angels, deities, ancestral guardians, and other entities as well.

I believe these issues are among the reasons why so many people today are turning to the Craft of the Wise, following a path that respects all life, all worlds, and all beings. A path of healing and growth. A path that offers peace, harmony, and joy. And I believe that's why the fae will decide to work with us, for our mutual benefit.

Now let's find out more about the different types of fairies, particularly the fae families in Celtic traditions. In the next chapter we'll consider their lineages, their individual characteristics, and what you need to know in order to work in partnership with them effectively and safely.

Chapter 2

THE DIFFERENT KINDS
OF FAIRIES

L ike humans, fairies have social strata—and the classes don't usually mix. They live in different places, engage in different pursuits, and play different roles in their own world as well as in ours. Different codes of conduct exist for dealing with fairies of various classes too, just as in the mortal realm—you wouldn't interact with the queen of England in the same way you would with one of her maids, nor should you treat the Fairy Queen like you might a domestic spirit. When you're working with the fae, it's good to know which folks you're dealing with and the rules of behavior associated with them.

> "We find in most countries a popular belief in different classes of beings distinct from men, and from the higher orders of divinities. These beings are usually believed to inhabit, in the caverns of the earth, or the depths of the waters, a region of their own. They generally excel mankind in power and in knowledge, and like them are subject to the inevitable laws of death, though after a more prolonged period of existence."
>
> **THOMAS KEIGHTLEY**, *Fairy Mythology*

In *Fairy and Folk Tales of the Irish Peasantry*, Irish poet William Butler Yeats described two groups known as solitary fairies and trooping fairies. Solitary fairies were considered the peasants, trooping fairies the aristocrats. Celtic fairies aren't the only ones to establish hierarchies, however. Norse myths speak of female protector spirits called *disir* who ranked below the *asyniur* deities. In Germanic legends we find housekeeping fairies known as *berchta*, as well as swan maidens who led warriors in battle.

This chapter will introduce you to a number of different types of fairies. You'll learn about their particular characteristics, abilities, and how they may be able to help you. As you'll soon see, fairies are as diverse as people. Among them you'll encounter Ireland's Tuatha dé Danann, who some sources say are the prototypes for human beings. You'll also meet the elemental spirits who take care of our planet. And, you'll gain insight into certain types of fairies with whom you may choose to work magick.

SOLITARY FAIRIES

As their name implies, solitary fairies prefer to reside alone instead of in communities, and they don't often interact with human beings. Consequently, you would be wise to leave them alone if you happen to stumble upon them in the wilds—although you probably won't see them if they don't want you to. If you try to get too friendly or don't respect their domain, they may play tricks on you, such as causing you to get lost. A German mountain fairy named Rübezahl was known to mislead hikers and travelers who wandered into his territory. Sometimes he conjured freak storms to frighten the intruders away.

Many nature spirits fall into this category. These solitary fairies guard and guide the lives of plants and animals, protect the forests and waterways, and can influence natural conditions on earth. Reclusive beings, they live in trees, caves, or barrows beneath hills, known in Ireland as *sidhe*. They come in a variety of shapes and sizes, and, like all fairies, they can change their appearance at will. Generally, they dress in simple, rustic clothing, often red, brown, or gray in color. Some, though, particularly those who make their homes in lakes and streams, may wear nothing at all.

> "The function of the nature spirits of woodland, meadow, and garden...
> is to furnish the vital connecting link between the stimulating energy of
> the sun and the raw material of the form. That growth of a plant which
> we regard as the customary and inevitable result of associating the three
> factors of sun, seed, and soil would never take place if the fairy builders
> were absent."
>
> EDWARD GARDNER,
> quoted in Sir Arthur Conan Doyle's *The Coming of the Fairies*

TROOPING FAIRIES

Trooping fairies got their name because they travel in long, elaborate processions throughout the countryside—sometimes numbering a hundred-strong—in which they ride on horseback or in chariots. Sociable and fun-loving, they're fond of parties, where they play music, dance, and dine like royalty. According to some Irish accounts, they descended from deities who reigned thousands of years ago, before mortals invaded their lands and forced the fae to retreat into the parallel world where they live today.

Like Medieval and Renaissance courts, these fairy families include kings and queens, knights, ladies-in-waiting, bards, and more. When they're not traveling about the countryside, trooping fairies live in castles on hilltops or under sacred lakes. They dress like royals too, in elegant gowns, rich fabrics, and showy jewelry. Despite the incursion of humans into their world, trooping fairies don't usually harm people and may even be willing to interact with them on occasion—so long as the people demonstrate adequate respect. That's not to say the fae won't play pranks on unwitting mortals, however. Watch your jewelry, for these clever folk will steal it if they can.

Fairy Sighting

English poet and artist William Blake claimed to have seen a fairy funeral in his garden. In his book *The Lives of the Most Eminent British Painters, Sculptors, and Architects*, Allan Cunningham quoted Blake as saying he observed "a procession of creatures of the size and colour of green and grey grasshoppers, bearing a body laid out on a rose-leaf, which they buried with songs, and then disappeared." Fairies live a very long time, but apparently they aren't immortal.

One of the most famous members of this class of fairies is Queen Mab, wife of the Fairy King Oberon—until Titania displaced her in Shakespeare's *A Midsummer Night's Dream.* In *Romeo and Juliet,* the Bard describes Mab as a diminutive pixie prankster who drives a chariot and plays tricks on men while they sleep. Ben Jonson, Percy Bysshe Shelley, Herman Melville, J.M. Barrie, Neil Gaiman, Jim Butcher, and numerous other noted authors have written about Queen Mab, picturing her as everything from mischievous to malevolent. In the Hellboy comic series, she's the queen of Ireland's Tuatha dé Danann and is married to their leader, Dagda, King of the Fairies.

You might want to invite a group of trooping fairies to join you in a festive ritual or celebration, especially at Beltane or Midsummer when the weather is nice. They're drawn to upbeat events with plentiful food and drink, music and dancing. Their presence can add a special, joyful exuberance to your gathering. Some witches who work with fairies say you shouldn't cast a circle around the place where you perform a ritual if you want to attract the fae—doing so will deter them from participating.

IRELAND'S TUATHA DÉ DANANN

Known as the children of the goddess Danu, these mythical entities are said to be the divine ancestors of the Irish people. Portrayed in legends as heroic beings, they ruled the Emerald Isle long before humans set foot there. Myths describe the Danann as a beautiful, highly intelligent, nearly immortal race—perhaps deities, perhaps fairies, perhaps superhumans—gifted in music, art, healing, poetry, and smithcraft. Of course, they possessed wondrous magickal talents as well.

Magick Tools

The Danann's four-principle magick tools bear similarities to those witches use today: the sword of Nuada that brought victory in battle; the cauldron of Dagda that constantly provided food; the spear of Lugh that always struck its mark; and the stone of destiny, called Lia Fail, that connected the Danann to the land.

Otherworldly in nature, they interacted with mortals and occasionally mated with them—until the thirteenth century B.C.E. when legends say warriors called the Milesians invaded Ireland and over-powered the Danann. After being defeated in battle, folklore tells us, the Danann retreated underground, or into a mystical realm known as the Otherworld, where they live to this day beneath sacred mounds called *sidhe* (pronounced *shee*). According to some sources, the Danann were gods and goddesses before the Milesian invasion but were demoted to fairies (called the *daoine sidhe*) afterward. Their great leader, Dagda, became King of the Fairies.

> "The gods of ancient mythology were changed into the demi-gods and heroes of ancient poetry, and these demi-gods again became, at a later age, the principal characters of our nursery tales."
>
> MAX MÜLLER, editor of *Sacred Books of the East*

SCOTLAND'S SEELIE AND UNSEELIE COURTS

Scottish mythology describes two fairy groups, one benevolent, one malevolent. The good guys are known as the Seelie Court—*seelie* translates to "happy," "blessed," or "fortunate." The bad actors are called the Unseelie Court, suggesting they lack the qualities of their nicer counterparts.

Legends give reports of the Seelie helping people and rewarding humans who display generosity toward the poor. Known as the fairies of the Summer Court, they're said to rule during the salubrious summer months. Beautiful and good-natured, they might play tricks on mortals, but they intend no real harm. The Unseelie, however, dislike people and may torment them, make them ill, or even strike them dead just for sport. Considered the fairies of the Winter Court, they reign during the harsh winter months.

The Queen of Air and Darkness

Jim Butcher, author of The Dresden Files series, names Queen Mab as a pow-erful ruler of the Unseelie Court and dubs her the Queen of Air and Dark-ness. In his stories, she lives in a castle made of ice, and she's as cold-hearted as her frozen domicile. Percy Bysshe Shelley paints her and her home in a more favorable light, however. According to the poet, the Fairy Queen lives on a golden island where she commands the stars and the oceans.

WALES'S TYLWYTH TEG

A race of beautiful fairies known as the Tylwyth Teg, which means "fair family," figures prominently in Welsh folklore. Good-natured and social, they live in clans and make their home in a magickal place called Annwn (a.k.a. the Otherworld). There the fae grow fabulous fruit trees and flowers, which once upon a time they shared with humans on Beltane (May 1). Legends say these fairies are generally accepting of people and sometimes marry mortals. However, the Tylwyth Teg also have a reputation for kidnapping male children, so don't leave your little boys alone with them.

Gerald of Wales

The oldest known account of the Tylwyth Teg comes from Giraldus Cambrensis (Gerald of Wales), who traveled through Wales with the Archbishop Baldwin of Canterbury in 1188. He described them in his *Itinerary of Giraldus Cambrensis* as handsome, supernatural beings, about 3 feet tall.

ELEMENTAL FAIRIES

You're quite likely already familiar with the four elements—earth, air, fire, and water—that are the building blocks of our earthly realm. You work with them in your magickal practice when you use your primary tools: the pentagram, athame, wand, and chalice, respectively. If you read tarot, you know that the four suits in the Minor Arcana correspond to these elements. If you practice astrology, you understand the groupings of zodiac signs into elemental categories.

> "Under the general designation of fairies and fays, these spirits of the elements appear in the myth, fable, tradition, or poetry of all nations, ancient and modern. Their names are legion—peris, devs, djins, sylvans, satyrs, fauns, elves, dwarfs, trolls, norns, hisses, kobolds, brownies, and many more. They have been seen, feared, blessed, banned, and invoked in every quarter of the globe and in every age."
>
> **MADAME HELENA BLAVATSKY,** *Isis Unveiled*

Fairies, too, have elemental affinities, based on their habitat, their characteristics, and the ways they function in our world. As a Wiccan, if you choose to engage the fae and establish a working relationship with them, you need to understand which elements they occupy and how the energies of the different elements will benefit your spellcraft.

Earth Fairies

Earth fairies, as you might expect, serve as Mother Earth's caretakers, overseeing the world's flowers, trees, crops, and other plants. Crystals and gemstones fall in their domain too. These hardworking spirits are responsible for the growth and well-being of plants—according to some sources, they provide the soul-energy botanicals need to thrive. They also help heal our planet from the destructive effects caused by humans. Earth fairies come in a wide range of sizes, shapes, and personalities, including pixies, sprites, gnomes, dryads, forest fairies, mountain fairies, and elves. If you practice herbal healing or botanical spells, or if you work with crystals, you'll want to get to know these fae folk better.

> "Fairies of the earth are caretakers of our soil, water and trees,
> They watch over beautiful creatures such as bears, bunnies and bees.
> Fairies ask that you breathe in and appreciate the vantage
> point from which you stand,
> Then trod carefully and respectfully with each intentional
> step you make across this beautiful land."
>
> MOLLY FRIEDENFELD, The Book of Simple Human Truths

Air Fairies

Also known as sylphs, air fairies guide the winds and clean up air pollution so we mortals can breathe. They also protect and direct birds, bats, and flying insects—you might even spot them on the wings of airplanes, keeping the occupants safe. Most winged fairies belong to this group. Witches associate the air element with communication, so these fairies can help you create effective affirmations and incantations.

Water Fairies

Undines, nymphs, merrows, sprites, and some mermaids fall into this fairy category. As you'd expect, they regulate the tides, direct the flow of rivers and streams, and bring the rains. Water fairies also protect fish and all forms of aquatic life. Although malevolent ones have been known to cause storms at sea and sink ships, others guide seafarers on safe journeys. If you concoct magick potions and lotions, ask these master formulators to share their secrets with you.

Fire Fairies

These spirits live in volcanoes and in the deserts of the world, but you may also find them in fireplaces, campfires, and candle flames. You might spot them in sunbeams and in lightning too. Some people who've seen these spirits describe them as resembling glowing lizards. Occult literature sometimes calls them salamanders. On occasion, these fairies spark fires that burn deadwood so that new growth can take place. When you do candle magick or fire rituals, invite these beings to lend their energy to your spellwork.

INCLUDING THE ELEMENTAL FAIRIES IN RITUALS

Usually we're not aware of the presence of elemental fairies at our rituals, but they might be there, just beyond the range of our vision. Witches often "call the quarters" at the start of a ritual and ask the guardians of the four directions to join in. As you probably know, each of the directions corresponds to an element: east to air, south to fire, west to water, and north to earth. The guardians provide protection and bring their special abilities to bear during the ritual.

You may choose to include the elemental fairies in your rituals as well. Most witches share a concern for the planet and its inhabitants with these nature spirits who care for our earth. Therefore, these fairies will probably agree to work with you for the common good. Use this simple method for calling them or design your own.

1. Start at the easternmost point of the sacred space where you will perform your ritual. Light incense to appeal to the air fairies. Say aloud:

> "FAIRIES OF AIR, SPIRITS OF COMMUNICATION, WE WELCOME YOU
> IN THIS SACRED SPACE. CARRY OUR WISHES FAR AND WIDE ON
> THE WINDS THAT BLOW AROUND THE WORLD."

2. Go to the southernmost point and light a candle to attract the fire fairies. Say aloud:

> "Fairies of fire, spirits of inspiration, we welcome you in this sacred space. Carry our wishes far and wide on the beams of light that shine upon the world."

3. Go to the westernmost point and set a bowl or chalice of water there to acknowledge the water fairies. Say aloud:

> "Fairies of water, spirits of imagination, we welcome you in this sacred space. Carry our wishes far and wide in the drops of rain that fall upon the world."

4. Go to the northernmost point and lay a crystal there for the earth fairies. Say aloud:

> "Fairies of earth, spirits of manifestation, we welcome you in this sacred space. Convey our wishes far and wide, in every grain of sand, every bit of loam that is our world."

At the end of the ritual, thank the fairies for their participation and send them on their way with a fond farewell.

FAIRY FRIENDS AND FOES

The myths of every culture throughout the world describe fairies of all sizes, shapes, colors, and abilities. Some are familiar to Westerners, such as leprechauns and elves. Others, particularly those found in Asian and African legends, may seem a bit strange to those of us who grew up with Tinker Bell as the fairy sine qua non.

Japan's Kappa

One of the oddest fairies of all is Japan's kappa, a chartreuse, flesh-eating water spirit with webbed feet and fish scales (or a turtle shell) covering his body. He has a hollow on the top of his head that holds a magick liquid that gives him strength. If you trick him into spilling the liquid, he forfeits his powers.

Flying fairies dominate the scene today, but they didn't really become popular until the Victorian era. J.M. Barrie's winged creation, Tinker Bell, made her debut in 1904 in the play *Peter Pan*, and she's dominated the scene ever since. Early legends, however, spoke of a variety of fae folk.

The fairies mentioned here come from Celtic mythology, because the practices of many modern-day Wiccans and neopagans derive from Celtic traditions. They're by no means the only fae who populate the legends and lore of Britain, Ireland, and other places where the Celts have left their mark, however. Additionally, each belief system and country, from China to Italy to Peru, has its own cast of characters, but I've limited this list because the fae folk are too numerous to include in a single book. Some of these beings are helper spirits who will agree to assist you in your magickal practice, assuming you compensate them adequately. Others you're better off leaving alone—be forewarned.

Pixies

Often described as small enough to sit on flower blossoms, these nature spirits fall into the category of "good guys." Artists depict them with pointy ears and wearing green outfits. Whenever you work plant magick or do herbal healing, you're likely to encounter these fairies. If you're a green witch or a gardener, you'll want to appease them and win their allegiance.

Elves

Before elves made their appearance in Celtic lore, they populated Norse and Germanic mythology. Some literature, such as J.R.R. Tolkien's Lord of the Rings trilogy, describes them as godlike, tall, and beautiful. Elsewhere these beings appear as dwarfs, like Snow White's seven companions, or as short, squat, mischievous creatures a.k.a. Santa's helpers. The Welsh adopted these fairies into their legends and called them *ellyll*. Elves are known for their skills as healers and artisans. If your magickal practice involves healing, you'll want to get on the good side of these guys. Sometimes they assist carpenters, metalsmiths, and craftspeople too. Solicit their aid if you want to build an altar, carve a magick wand, or make gemstone talismans and amulets.

Food for Fairies

We can see the age-old custom of leaving food and libation for the fairies in our present-day practice of putting out milk and cookies for Santa Claus (who, after all, is sometimes referred to as a "jolly old elf") in exchange for the gifts he brings. Of course, Santa's origins are rooted in the folklore of northern Europe, in the mythological person of St. Nicholas.

Leprechauns

Entrenched in Irish folklore, leprechauns are usually thought of as little old men with green coats and funny hats who smoke briar pipes. Often they work day jobs as cobblers. These solitary fairies are notorious tricksters who, legends say, will hand over a pot of gold if you manage to trap them. But that's no easy task, and it's unlikely you'll outwit these clever characters. They can help you with prosperity magick, but be careful to cover all your bases when working with these crafty fairies, or you may end up with coal instead of gold in your pockets. Don't solicit their aid in dubious activities or get-rich-quick schemes—and be sure to share your bounty with them.

Boston Celtics

The Boston Celtics basketball team chose the leprechaun as their mascot, hoping he'd bring them good luck. Their logo shows him wearing a shamrock-patterned vest and bow tie, smoking a pipe while leaning on a shillelagh, spinning a basketball on his finger, and winking to let you know he's got everything in hand.

Brownies

These household fairies have long been welcome in the homes of Celtic people, for they come in during the night and tidy up while the residents sleep. Similar to the German kobolds, they're short in stature, modest, and hardworking. But if you offend them, legends say, they'll break dishes, spill milk, and chase off livestock. They may also be responsible for those mysterious noises that keep you awake at night. Brownies can help you with domestic chores as well as tasks that seem tedious or physically demanding. They can provide endurance and focus in work-related endeavors as well. Don't treat them like low-level hired hands, however—they're magickal beings, not servants.

Grogoches

Said to be part fairy and part human, these scruffy-looking little guys are found in Irish and Scottish legends. They appear to be covered either with brownish fur or a mat of twigs and leaves, rather than clothes. Although grogoches are usually solitary fairies, they'll perform household chores for people they like, such as cleaning the kitchen or weeding the garden. They work cheap too. Just give them fresh cream to thank them for helping out.

Merrows

These Irish water spirits look like beautiful women, except for the webbing between their fingers. Although the ocean is their natural home, these fairies—who are among the more sociable of the fae folk—sometimes come on land to mingle with human beings. When they do, they must remove their cloaks or red caps—and if a person snatches those garments the merrows can't return to the water. Legends say merrows possess great wealth, having scavenged treasure from sunken ships. Therefore, they can bring gold, jewels, and other riches your way if you manage to win their favor. Irish folklore is full of stories about fishermen capturing and marrying these female fairies. But if a merrow ever finds her cloak or cap, she'll immediately go back to the sea, leaving her human husband and mixed-race children behind.

Korrigans

Korrigans are popular figures in Breton folklore. These female fairies, similar to the Welsh *gwragedd annwn*, live near lakes and streams where they lure men they desire by enticing them to drink from their magickal waters. Some tales say korrigans abduct human babies and raise them as their own. The Lady of the Lake in the Arthurian legends is thought by some to have been a korrigan. Although these seductive fairies can give you tips for working sex magick, be very careful dealing with them—you may end up binding yourself in the process.

Bean sidhe (banshee)

Bean sidhe means "fairy woman" in Gaelic. This female spirit later became known in Scottish folklore as a prognosticator of death, recognized by her chilling, high-pitched wail. She often wears a gray hooded cloak and shows up at the home of someone who is destined to die soon—although she doesn't cause the person's demise. Other accounts liken her to the Scottish *bean nighe*, a spirit-woman who washes the bloody clothes of a person who's about to die, also called the Washer at the Stream. Sometimes she's considered an ancestor spirit. Although she's often a frightening figure, the *bean sidhe* can help people prepare for the passing of loved ones or their own transitions, sort of like a fairy hospice worker. Because she journeys between this world and the hereafter, the *bean sidhe* may also assist you in communicating with those who now reside on the Other Side.

A Personal Bean Sidhe

Some of the old Irish families are said to have their very own personal *bean sidhe*, who lets them know when a relative is about to pass over. In the highly acclaimed Disney movie *Darby O'Gill and the Little People* (1959) starring Sean Connery, a *bean sidhe* makes a terrifying and unforgettable appearance.

Dullahans

In Irish folklore, the dullahan is a terrifying figure and a harbinger of death. In his hands he carries his own dismembered head, which glows in the dark like a lantern, while riding a shadowy horse with flaming nostrils. In some tales, he drives a death coach drawn by six ghostly steeds. Like the *bean sidhe*, he shows up at the home of someone who will soon die or at the site where a fatal event will occur imminently. The dullahan appears as the Headless Horseman in Washington Irving's story "The Legend of Sleepy Hollow." This is one fairy you don't want to mess with! If you see his apparition, draw the curtains and cover your ears with your hands, lest you hear him call your name.

Pookas

These Irish mischief-makers like to shapeshift into animals or birds, especially horses. At night, pookas roam about damaging crops, scaring livestock, and vandalizing property. According to some tales, they like to take people on midnight rides—but don't go, it could be dangerous. Although it may seem useless, or worse, to associate with these rogues, they can be assets in extreme situations when you need to protect your territory or guard against enemies—but you'll need to bribe them and guide them with a firm hand.

ANIMAL FAIRIES

Fairies frequently shapeshift into animals and birds—they can take pretty much any form they like, even appearing as mythical creatures like unicorns and dragons. The Irish selkies live as seals in the ocean but change into human beings when they come on land. The Welsh gwyllion sometimes assume goat forms. Celtic tales describe deer as supernatural creatures—the god Cernunnos is depicted with a stag's antlers on his head. The Greek goddess Artemis usually appears with a deer as a companion, and in Norse myths the red deer is viewed as a messenger between the Otherworld and the earth. Stories also speak of fairies milking cattle and riding horses. Some animal fairies may agree to assist you; others may be dangerous or destructive.

Magick Cats

Fairies and witches have long been known to keep cats as familiars (magickal companions who participate in spellcraft), and legends say witches frequently shapeshift into cats. Because cats are nocturnal creatures, many people find them mysterious—black cats, in particular, seem to disappear in the darkness. During the Burning Times in Europe, tens of thousands of people were accused of witchcraft and executed, along with countless cats that were thought to be witches in disguise.

But throughout history, cats have been revered by many. The Celts attributed supernatural powers to felines. In Irish and Scottish folklore, large black fairy cats guard the Underworld and its treasure. Magickal white cats accompany the Welsh goddess Cerridwen wherever she goes. Gray cats pull the chariot of the Norse goddess Freya. The ancient Egyptians worshipped cats as deities, including the cat goddess Bast and the half-feline, half-human goddess Sekhmet. Waving cats known as *maneki neko* bring good fortune to Chinese and Japanese homes. Maybe your feline friend is actually a fairy in disguise! Even if you don't share your home with a flesh-and-blood cat, you can invite a fairy cat to lend you her stealth, grace, cleverness, and night vision.

Black Dogs

The folklore of the British Isles and Ireland speak of shaggy black canines as big as calves. Often stories link these dogs with death, and, like the *bean sidhe*, they appear when someone is about to pass. Some accounts say they're demons or ghosts, whereas other tales describe them as fairies. A type of fairy called a bogie often shows up as a black dog. In Scottish folklore, black dogs are said to guard treasure—perhaps fairy treasure—much as the cat *sidhe* do in Ireland. Although legends usually warn people to steer clear of these magickal dogs, who can be vicious, if one of them takes a liking to you it can protect you and your home. Just don't expect it to fetch or roll over on command.

Enchanted Horses

Considering the fairies' fascination with all things equine, it's no surprise to find horses in fairyland, and fairies posing as horses. The Welsh goddess Rhiannon is a noted shapeshifter who likes to take the form of a swift white horse and lead humans on a merry chase. Pixies, in particular, are said to "borrow" horses for midnight rides. In 2009, the UK's *Bridport News* reported that throughout rural Britain people were discovering their horses' manes and tails mysteriously braided, but no horses were harmed or stolen. Nobody could figure out who did it, why, or how. Could fairies have been responsible?

Fairy Horses

In the fairy funeral procession poet and artist William Blake witnessed, many of the fae sat astride miniature horses; others rode in chariots drawn by fairy steeds. Herbie Brennan, author of The Faerie Wars Chronicles series of books, claims he saw two dozen white horses "no bigger than cocker spaniels" gallop across the Longstone Rath, a national monument located in County Tipperary, Ireland, on Samhain, 1971.

If you win the respect of a fairy horse, it may offer you gifts of speed and strength. Or, it may show up to encourage you to be more playful, to step away from the computer and experience the freedom of riding across the countryside with the wind at your back. Beware the Scottish water horse called a kelpie, though. Considered to be a member of the Unseelie Court, these malevolent fairies invite mortals to go for a leisurely canter. At the end of the ride, however, the kelpies drag their unsuspecting victims into the water where they kill and eat them.

Now that you've met some of the fae, let's consider the ethics, etiquette, and practices associated with them. If you planned to visit a foreign country, you'd familiarize yourself with the customs and rules of that country, right? Otherwise, you might inadvertently ruin your chances of an enjoyable journey or offend the very folks you want to please. The same holds true when you visit fairyland.

Chapter 3

CAUTIONS AND CAVEATS FOR WORKING WITH FAIRIES

Y ou probably wouldn't invite a person you'd just met on an online dating site to come to your home, and you should be equally discriminating when welcoming fairies into your house, garden, or workplace. Not all fairies have your best interests in mind. Truth be told, most fairies don't like mortals, even Wiccans, and consider us an inferior race. The spriggans, for instance, serve as fairy police, meting out punishments to humans who have displeased the fae. Goblins go around trashing property and harassing humans, just because they can. But if you've decided it's worth your while to work with fairy helpers—and you can certainly reap benefits from collaborating with them—exercise caution.

In this chapter you'll learn about some of the characteristics, behaviors, and conceptions commonly associated with the fae folk. The fairy world is populated by many diverse beings, some relatively benevolent, some downright dangerous. Let's consider some ways to optimize your success and minimize the risks involved in partnering with fairies.

FAIRY CHARACTERISTICS

Fairies don't hold the same values or follow the same codes of ethics that humans do. They're amoral, concerned mainly with what serves their needs or pleasures. Human beings may commit crimes or act badly toward their fellow beings, but they usually know they're going against the accepted rules of their society. Fairies don't. For the most part they don't feel emotions in the way humans do. When they behave vindictively toward people who offend them, they're not acting out of anger as we know it; they're simply bringing justice to those who've wronged them. Their purpose is rectification and restoring order—and their dispassion can enable them to act at times with what we might consider great cruelty. Even helpful fae folk will play pranks on people, just for the fun of it.

> "The faery beings are potentially powerful allies, yet if you enter their realm for the wrong reasons, may become terrible opponents....Everything in the faery realm is intensified, amplified, sometimes painfully or ecstatically real."
>
> R.J. STEWART, *Earth Light*

Romantic relationships with fae folk can be especially dicey. Many fairies are seductive and licentious, and accounts of them mating with humans abound in folklore. Beautiful females, such as the Breton korrigans and the Irish merrows, use their abundant charms—and their magick—to lure men they desire. But don't expect a fling with a fairy to last. The fae don't understand commitment, certainly not to humans. Once they've finished with their mortal partners, they'll dump their hapless mates and go on their way.

The German nixies use their enchanting voices to entice mortals. These beguiling beauties may marry men, but they may also drown them. The Russian rusalki are even more dangerous. These lustful water spirits take human form in order to party with handsome young men for the night—then they dance their mates to death or drown them.

Shapeshifters and Tricksters

You may think you're interacting with a human being—or an animal, a bird, or a plant—only to discover it's really a fairy in disguise. All fairies can shapeshift. And all are tricksters. They especially like snatching and hiding things from us, either to get our attention or for their own amusement. Many fairies just like to tease us, but others have nefarious intentions. Will-o'-the-wisps, who appear as flickering lights in the Welsh bogs and woods at night, lead travelers astray, never to be seen or heard from again.

DO'S AND DON'TS WHEN DEALING WITH FAIRIES

As we've already discussed, it's never a good idea to offend the fae. If you cross them, they'll get revenge. Legends warn us not to call them by name—doing so presumes a level of familiarity to which humans aren't entitled, and which the fairies consider disrespectful. Instead, our ancestors referred to them euphemistically as the Gentry, Good People, or the Good Neighbors.

If you want to meet the fae, you must allow them to come to you. Don't go chasing them into the woods or water—you may risk your life in the attempt. Don't try to trap them either. Fairy tales say that if you capture a leprechaun he'll give you a pot of gold in exchange for his freedom. But your chances of outsmarting a fairy are slim to nil. First of all, they're psychic. Second, they've lived hundreds, maybe thousands of years, and have garnered plenty of wisdom and experience during that time.

Leprechaun Trickery

One story tells of an Irishman who managed to nab a leprechaun. The fairy agreed to pay the man a ransom, and indicated that his pot of gold was buried beneath a thistle bush. To mark the spot, the leprechaun tied a red scarf around the thistle, while the young man went home to get a shovel. When he returned, he saw red scarves tied on all the thistles in the field—the man had no idea where to dig for the treasure.

Fairies don't do favors for mortals out of the goodness of their hearts—we don't even know for sure if the fae have hearts. They'll agree to help you only if there's something in it for them. Offer them gifts in return for their services, and remember to thank them. Many fairies are attracted to bright, shiny objects, such as jewelry, glass balls, or other baubles. According to some sources, though, fairies dislike elaborate displays of gratitude—simply leave their "payment" and go on your way.

Food and drink rank among the most popular offerings for fairies. In early agrarian societies, farmers frequently left bowls of milk, glasses of mead, or loaves of bread for the fae to prevent them from harming crops and livestock. Modern-day fairies still enjoy milk, beer, wine, fruit, or a plate of whatever you're eating for supper. They're particularly fond of sweets—cake, cookies, candy, and especially honey. Organic foods are best—remember, fairies protect nature; consequently they're opposed to chemical fertilizers and pesticides. And if you offer them GMO products you're asking for trouble.

Although feeding the fairies is a good way to thank them, don't accept food or beverages from them. Legends warn that anyone who eats or drinks with the fae will slip into their realm and be trapped there forever. Time in fairyland bears no similarity to what we experience in our own world—5 minutes there might equal fifty years here—so while you're enjoying a fairy feast, you don't realize life on earth has passed by without you.

Rip Van Winkle

Washington Irving's story "Rip Van Winkle" is a good example of the caveat against accepting a dinner invitation from the fae. In it, Rip meets a bunch of short, bearded fellows playing ninepins in New York's Catskill Mountains. The creatures—most likely dwarves, elves, or gnomes—share a libation with him, after which he falls asleep and doesn't wake up until twenty earth years later.

FAIRY THIEVES

If a fairy sees something she wants, she'll "appropriate" it without worrying whether the item belongs to someone else. Fairies don't subscribe to the same rules and ethics we do, remember, and they certainly don't feel obliged to respect human laws. If you notice that objects around your house have "gone missing" it could mean a fairy found them appealing and snagged them for herself. Jewelry is particularly susceptible to fairy filching. Who among us hasn't lost an earring mysteriously? (Tip: Save those solo earrings to offer as thank-you gifts for fairies later on.) But the fae may also snatch eyeglasses, keys, clothing, hairbrushes, kitchen gadgets—whatever they need or fancy.

The Borrowers

In her award-winning children's book *The Borrowers*, first published in 1952, English author Mary Norton wrote about a family of little people, known as the Borrowers, who lived in the walls of a house and stole things they needed from the human occupants, the Big People. The book became so popular that it spun off a series of five novels as well as several TV series and movies.

Sometimes the fae steal things for their own amusement, such as the pixies who like to borrow horses for nighttime rides. But in some instances, they may be trying to get your attention. If you notice certain types of objects disappearing, consider whether there's a connection. Vanishing books may be the fairies' way of nudging you to study new subjects. Missing garden tools may mean the fae want you to tend to your flowers and shrubs. After my ex-husband and I split up, the necklace I'd worn on my wedding day mysteriously disappeared from a hiding place no human knew about. I took this as a sign from the fairies that I needed to let go of the past.

Usually, fairy thieves don't intend any harm. Ask them nicely to return the item they've absconded with, and offer to trade something else if they give it back.

CHANGELINGS

Of all fairy thefts, child abductions were what our ancestors feared most. Folklore abounds with tales of "changelings," fae children that the fairies considered substandard and swapped for human babies. The fairies supposedly snuck into nurseries at night, where they traded their weaklings for healthy mortal children—unbeknownst to the parents, who might not discover the exchange for months or even years. It's said the fae even cast what's known as a "glamour" (a magickal illusion) on blocks of wood to make them look like babies and left them in cradles to deceive the parents.

According to some legends, fairies need to replenish the bloodlines of their race periodically, and they seek human infants for that purpose. In Europe during the Medieval and Renaissance periods, children born with physical or mental disabilities, or those who had diseases that couldn't be explained, were thought to be changelings. Martin Luther, leader of the Protestant Reformation, believed in the idea of changelings and wrote that children with abnormalities should be left out in the woods to perish.

Child Sacrifices

Celtic folklore says the fae were required to pay a blood tithe every seven years, in order to preserve and strengthen their clan. The payment was a child. Instead of giving up their own, the fairies stole mortal youngsters to sacrifice. The ballad of Tam Lin, a human man who lived many years in fairyland, describes this ancient rite and tells how a human woman confronts the Fairy Queen in order to rescue the captured mortal Tam Lin from certain death.

GETTING RID OF FAIRIES

Thus far, we've been discussing how you can interact with fairies safely and productively. But what if you think fairies have intruded into your life and you don't want them there? Maybe you're tired of having your jewelry disappear or being awakened at night by mysterious banging noises. Maybe fairies are disrupting your magickal activities.

Our ancestors believed fairies recoiled from the sound of church bells. Loud chimes, too, irritate their sensitive hearing. Celtic people throughout history have hung rowan branches above their doorways to guard against intruders. Folklore tells us fairies flee from iron, which may explain the old practice of hanging an iron horseshoe above the door to your home. Placing iron tongs beside a cradle was said to prevent the fae from snatching a baby. An iron lock on a stable door kept them from stealing horses.

Sprinkling salt in the corners of your home is a popular way to protect against unwanted spirits of any kind. You can also fashion magick amulets to safeguard your home and loved ones—Chapter 8 includes suggestions for creating these, along with other protection spells. Sometimes all you have to do is tell the fairies to go away. Unless you have something they want, they probably won't hang around where they're not welcome.

If you do choose to meet and collaborate with the fae folk, read on.

SHAMANIC JOURNEYING TO THE LAND OF THE FAE

Shamanic journeying is an important part of working magick with fairies. Shamanic traditions exist in all cultures—the Celts, the native tribes of the Americas, the indigenous people of Australia and New Zealand—and probably have since human beings first set foot on this planet. Caitlin and John Matthews, in their book *The Encyclopaedia of Celtic Wisdom*, describe shamanism as "a worldwide practice in which the spiritual interrelationship of the earth with the otherworlds forms an interwoven fabric of physical and psychic being, affecting all forms of life, both seen and unseen."

What Are Shamans?

Certain individuals, known as shamans, possess special gifts, sensitivities, and powers that enable them to "walk between the worlds" and interact with the entities who reside there. Druids, seers, visionary poets, divinely inspired teachers, witches, pagan priests and priestesses, medicine men and women fall into this category. Often they embark on their spirit journeys via trance, induced by meditative techniques, magickal practices or rites, music and drumming, mind-altering substances, or other means. While entranced, they travel to myriad levels of existence in order to gain the knowledge that resides in other realities. Shamans then bring back foresight, healing, guidance, and wisdom to human beings. Some myths portray this in terms of a ritualistic sacrifice, such as that of the Norse god Odin, who hung on the great tree Yggdrasil for nine days in order to gain the wisdom of the runes for humanity.

When you go on a shamanic journey, you travel in mind, in imagination, in spirit. The places you're visiting aren't physical in the way our earthly realm is, so you don't need a corporeal body when you go there. You'll probably be aware of your physical body, but it's not relevant to your otherworldly experience. As is the case in dreams, you clearly witness and feel the spirit environment you're in and interact keenly with entities you meet there. You may even have sensations such as heat and cold. However, your physical form remains behind, right where you left it. And no, you won't get lost or stuck in another level of reality, so long as you take precautions. If you like, you can invite one of your spirit guides, guardians, angels, or animal helpers to go along with you for protection and direction.

Journeys Into Outer Space

Several years ago, I took a shamanic journey with a spirit guide to Titan, one of Saturn's moons. I knew virtually nothing about Titan or what to expect. As I approached, I saw it as a bright blue orb glowing against the black backdrop of space. When I slid into it, the sphere grew darker and denser—and it felt icy cold. The color and heavy pressure reminded me of being deep underwater. I sensed both actual water and a resonance I associated with water. It felt a bit overwhelming, as if I were in a small boat bobbing about on big waves. Streaking through the inky water were glowing chartreuse ripples that looked like phosphorescence: the entities that live there.

When I returned from my visit, I looked up Titan online and learned that it's composed primarily of water—ice mainly, and liquid methane lakes. It's believed to be the only heavenly body other than earth with stable bodies of water. It also has a dense atmosphere twice as thick as earth's—exactly what I'd experienced. According to www.space.com: "There is also data that suggests the presence of a liquid ocean beneath the surface."

On another occasion, I journeyed to the Pleiades. I'd intentionally avoided researching these celestial bodies so I could visit them with an open mind, without preconceptions that might influence my experience. As we drew near, my spirit guide told me the cluster known as the Seven Sisters had formed from the explosion of a single star, and explained that the stars were slowly moving apart.

To me the stars looked like incredibly brilliant blue-white diamonds scattered on a black velvet cloth. As we neared the archipelago, however, I noticed the stars were actually different colors, albeit very pale. More surprising, each resonated with a particular musical note. I wondered if this was what the "music of the spheres" meant—except they weren't spheres—they appeared jagged and a bit spiky. Some even seemed to have holes in them that made me think of open mouths. I chose to move in and get a closer look at one that glowed with a hint of orange, although the color wasn't consistent—part was yellowish, and a faint olive band wound around it. It resonated with the musical note D. My guide told me one reason shamans journey to these stars is to learn how to heal with sound.

When I returned, I went to the website EarthSky.org and read that astronomers believe the Pleiades star cluster formed from the same gas/dust cloud about one hundred million years ago. Other studies say the stars are physically related and move as a group, but they won't be held together by gravity forever and will eventually disperse. Though described as blue-white, a NASA image shows the stars as being of various colors, including orange—the star I'd chosen to observe is called Alcyone. Next, I brought up a music website and listened to the notes of the scale. The tone I remembered hearing was, indeed, D. Interestingly, Eastern healing philosophy connects that note with the human body's sacral chakra, and that chakra supposedly glows with orange light.

Shapeshifting

Shamans sometimes shapeshift into animals, birds, or other creatures in order to journey to the spirit worlds. In some instances, the reason for this is to bring the distinctive characteristics and powers of a particular creature along for learning, protection, guidance, or another purpose.

According to some sources, Celtic shamans choose to shapeshift into animals for a number of motives. They may desire to learn from the animal's spirit. They might want to avoid detection, and therefore take on a disguise that allows them to remain hidden. If the place the shaman is visiting is dangerous for humans, shapeshifting into an animal can provide safety. A shaman may seek to watch someone, unbeknownst to the observed, and masquerading as an animal allows that. Or, the shaman may wish to serve as a spirit animal guide or guardian for someone else. I'm sure there are other reasons too, and various shamanic traditions may have different objectives.

Shamans can shapeshift into a wide range of forms, including imaginary creatures such as dragons and unicorns. Some do it for deceptive or harmful reasons. But if you choose to engage in this magickal practice, it's best to do so for the benefit of others as well as for your own advantage, and not to get swept away by the heady power that can accompany the endeavor.

Cerridwen and Gwion

The story of the Celtic goddess Cerridwen and a boy named Gwion is an example of shapeshifting and shamanic journeying for the purpose of gaining knowledge. According to myth, the goddess instructed the boy to stir a magick potion she was concocting, but he ruined it. Afraid Cerridwen would be angry, Gwion shapeshifted into a hare in an attempt to hide from her. Of course, being a goddess, she wasn't fooled. She turned herself into a greyhound and pursued him. Gwion tried to escape by shifting into a fish. Cerridwen transformed herself into an otter and continued the pursuit. When he changed into a bird, she became a hawk. In desperation, Gwion took the form of a kernel of corn; Cerridwen shapeshifted into a hen and ate him. The magick grain grew inside her and was reborn as her son.

Can anyone become a shaman? In my opinion, the answer is yes, just as anyone can become a witch. We're all intuitive beings. We all have powers we've yet to recognize or use. We've all experienced journeying in one form or another, most commonly in dreams. Intention is the key factor. If you truly desire to expand your consciousness and believe it's possible, you can. Some people are naturally more talented than others, just as some of us have more musical or athletic talent than others. With practice and dedication, however, you can develop your innate ability and learn to temporarily leave behind your ordinary perception and soar into the unseen worlds.

BEFORE YOU JOURNEY TO FAIRYLAND

Before you set off for the land of the fae, take some time to determine why you want to enter their homeland. What do you hope to gain? What expectations do you have? Are there certain fairies you'd like to meet? What preparations are you willing to make? What method do you plan to use to journey? Have you done shamanic journeying before? Have you shapeshifted before? What did you experience?

> "[The faery realm] is not simply something that we imagine, for it has a true nature and firm identity of its own, existing even if you never think of it. The inhabitants of the faery realm are beautiful and terrible, inspiring and disturbing. If you go there, you will emerge changed."
>
> R.J. STEWART, *Earth Light*

Preparing for a trip to fairyland isn't the same as packing for a camping trip or a vacation at a fancy resort. Naturally, you don't have to take along any luggage, and reservations aren't required. You won't need a GPS or tourist guides either. However, it can be beneficial to schedule your forays at a prescribed time—especially if you opt to journey regularly. That way your mind and mood will begin to anticipate the shift from the mundane to the magickal world and adjust accordingly.

I've discussed the need for protection before, but I'm going to say it again. Entering other realms of existence, and the fairy realm in particular, brings risks as well as opportunities. For one thing, the world the fae inhabit is simultaneously more subtle and more intense than ours. Your sense of time, space, distance, and all the other perceptions and dimensions and distinctions you're accustomed to on earth will be drastically altered there. You'll encounter many things that appear strange—some beguiling, some frightening—and nothing is quite what it seems, at least when viewed through the lens of our physical world. Furthermore, the realm of the fae includes more than one "place," and each has its own nature.

As a witch, you're familiar with protection magick. You probably wear a pentagram. You know how to cast a circle and likely do so before you enact a spell or ritual. By the way, some practitioners of Fairy Witchcraft argue against circle-casting when working with the fae. They suggest you need to allow these spirits to enter your sacred space unhampered, in order to let them partner with you in performing magick. I can see both sides of the argument, and leave it to you to decide what you feel is best for you.

I always recommend doing some sort of protection magick before you engage with the fae, just as I always wear my seatbelt when I'm driving. I also do a quick protection visualization every time I slide behind the steering wheel of my car. In both cases, the protection doesn't prevent me from following my path, but it gives me a little added safety. The precautions also remind me that my actions involve a degree of risk and I need to stay alert.

- The simplest spell you can do is to surround yourself with pure white light before you perform any magick act. You may want to do this for protection in mundane matters too. But despite its simplicity, this oft-used spell is quite powerful.

- Wearing a pentagram is a familiar form of protection magick that won't stifle your rapport with the fairies. As a symbol of the earth element, it also helps to ground you when you're roaming about in the spirit world.

- Basil is a well-known herb of protection. Carry fresh or dried basil leaves in your pocket, or dab a little basil essential oil on your seven major chakra points before taking a meeting with the fae.

- Program a crystal to provide protection. Carry it with you when you go journeying into the unfamiliar territory of the fae—fairies love crystals and will recognize their power.

- Stay alert. This is easier said than done when you're in the presence of fairies, for they can be beguiling, seductive, and manipulative. However, the same advice holds true when you're walking in their world as when you're walking on an unfamiliar city street at night. Watch, listen, pay attention to hunches and instincts, and don't show fear.

In Chapter 8, I offer a number of protection spells, including instructions for making an amulet to keep you safe when you're working with the fairies. This amulet is designed to help you stay connected to the earth plane when you venture out into the spirit realms, and to guard against both physical and nonphysical dangers.

In Part Two of this book, you'll find some exercises to facilitate shamanic journeying and shapeshifting. These are practices that I've used successfully, but I recommend you also read books by various authors, listen to podcasts, attend classes or workshops, and/or explore the work of those who've gone before you—doing so will help you gain valuable insights and avoid mishaps. Techniques that work well for one person may not be the best ones for another individual.

In the next chapter we'll talk about where, when, and how to make contact with the fairies. We'll also look more closely at the Otherworld, the Underworld, and other places where fairies reside—and how to access them.

Chapter 4

WHERE TO MEET FAIRIES

Fairies live in a nonphysical world that parallels and intersects our own. Most of the time we can't see them. But periodically, when conditions are right, you may catch a fleeting glimpse of flickering lights that seem to have no source, or see an indistinct shape that magickally appears and then disappears just as quickly. You might even spot a full-blown figure of a mysterious supernatural being and interact with it, as countless people throughout history have done.

FAIRIES EXIST

The first step to meeting fairies is to accept that they exist. Perhaps you've heard the expression "You'll see it when you believe it." This certainly applies when you're dealing with the fae folk. Scientific and materialistic thinking reject the reality of things that can't be measured, weighed, or otherwise quantified in mechanical terms. But you can't subscribe to that philosophy if you hope to engage with beings who aren't physical. You have to accept, as Shakespeare wrote in *Hamlet*, "There are more things in heaven and earth...than are dreamt of in your philosophy."

In this chapter we'll talk about where fairies live, as well as when and where you are most likely to find them. You'll also learn a bit about their affinities with certain land formations, both natural and humanmade, such as fairy rings and megalithic sites like

Stonehenge. Additionally, we'll discuss the three worlds of existence, according to Celtic mythology, and the World Tree that connects our earth to the spirit realms. Finally, you'll be introduced to the wisdom of trees and the magickal language and oracle based on trees, known as Ogham.

The Colors of Fairies

In his book *The Coming of the Fairies*, Sir Arthur Conan Doyle, who wrote the Sherlock Holmes series, cited Charles W. Leadbeater's varied descriptions and experiences with fairies. "In England the emerald-green kind is probably the commonest, and I have seen it also in the woods of France and Belgium, in far-away Massachusetts, and on the banks of the Niagara river. The vast plains of the Dakotas are inhabited by a black-and-white kind which I have not seen elsewhere, and California rejoices in a lovely white-and-gold species which also appears to be unique."

WOODLANDS, LAKES, AND OTHER PLACES IN NATURE

Because many fairies are nature spirits, it stands to reason that you'll be more likely to meet them on a remote hiking trail in the mountains or beside a secluded pond in a pastoral setting than at your local mall. Therefore, you may want to designate a period of time each day, or as often as possible, to spend in nature, attuning your senses to the natural world. It's best to go fairy-hunting alone, for these sensitive creatures abhor crowds.

> "A lady, with whom I was riding in the forest, said to me, that the woods always seemed to her to wait, as if the genii who inhabit them suspended their deeds until the wayfarer has passed onward: a thought which poetry has celebrated in the dance of the fairies, which breaks off on the approach of human feet."
>
> **RALPH WALDO EMERSON, "History"**

Even if you live in a city, you can escape to a public park. Or, you might be able to create a container garden on your fire escape. Caring for plants in your home can encourage fairies to visit you too. Not only will this bring you into a closer relationship with Mother Earth, it will also sharpen your awareness and enable you to commune with the entities who care for our planet.

When you go on your excursions into nature, bring food for the fairies. Leave it on a tree stump, a rock, an earthen mound, or another place where the fae are sure to find it. Pick up any trash you see along the way. Tidy up the area, perhaps by gathering sticks and deadwood and stacking them neatly. If the fairies notice your efforts, they'll be more likely to consider you an ally than an adversary.

> "Faeries, come take me out of this dull world,
> For I would ride with you upon the wind,
> Run on the top of the dishevelled tide,
> And dance upon the mountains like a flame."
>
> **WILLIAM BUTLER YEATS,** *The Land of Heart's Desire*

STONE CIRCLES

England's Neolithic stone circles Stonehenge and Avebury, and Scotland's Ring of Brodgar, are famous for their magickal and mystical properties. According to Aubrey Burl's gazetteer, more than 1,300 stone circles exist in England, Scotland, Wales, Ireland, and Brittany. But these aren't the only places where early people built stone circles for purposes that still intrigue and mystify us today. Scandinavia, Poland, Syria, Hong Kong, Japan, Australia, and many other parts of the world also feature stone circles. Atlit Yam, off the coast of Israel, has an underwater one that dates back more than eight thousand years. As you might expect, these ancient monuments are favorite hangouts for fairies.

If you're fortunate enough to visit any of these sites, you'll probably experience something very special, maybe supernatural. But you may not have to travel that far to witness a fairy sighting. Many people have reported spotting fairies in smaller, less-well-known stone circles too. Years ago, I built a 28-foot-diameter stone labyrinth in the woods behind my home in Massachusetts. I regularly saw and sensed fairies there, both in the daytime and at night. They especially liked joining me when I performed rituals in my stone circle. Occasionally, intuitive friends witnessed them there as well.

Labyrinths

A labyrinth—not to be confused with a maze—has a single, winding pathway that leads into the center of the circular pattern and back out again. Walking a labyrinth symbolizes the journey to your own center and/or to the Source, and doing so can induce receptive states of consciousness. We find these elegant creations throughout the world—many date back thousands of years. Fairies are drawn to what's known as the seven-circuit labyrinth, because it emphasizes balance between humanity and nature. Chartres-style labyrinths? Not so much, probably because they're associated with Christianity and with relationships in the human community.

If you happen upon a stone circle, whether it appears to be naturally occurring or formed by human hands, stop, look, and listen. Allow your mind to grow quiet, your gaze to soften. If you're patient, you may see a fairy within the circle, watching you.

CROP CIRCLES

Who creates the mysterious, intricate designs known as crop circles? How? And why? For decades we've heard tales of intricate, geometric patterns appearing overnight in fields of grain, in countries around the world. Scientists and skeptics discount them as the work of humans, not supernatural beings, yet convincing answers to these questions remain elusive. The controversy continues, and crop circles fascinate us to this day.

Fairies in the Corn

Kornbachs, fairies found in the folklore of northern and eastern Europe, are said to resemble goats. They live in cornfields, hence their name, as well as fields of wheat, rye, and other types of grain. Are these spirits responsible for making crop circles? During the harvest season, reapers destroy the fairies' outdoor homes, so they must come indoors for the winter, where they serve as house fairies temporarily. According to legends, if the fairies are treated well, they'll bless the fields in the spring and foster a bountiful crop.

Crop circles aren't new, however. Ancient legends mention them, referring to them as "fairy circles." Supposedly, fairies dancing in fields of wheat, barley, flaxseed, rapeseed, and other crops—especially during midsummer in England—flattened the grain into beautiful designs. Today, as in our ancestors' time, eyewitnesses describe unexplained orbs of light floating above fields where crop circles appear. Are these lights the fairies admiring their work?

Peasant Protesters

In sixteenth-century France, crop circles were believed to be created by peasant farmers protesting their lot at the hands of the aristocracy. The saboteurs trampled crops at night, wearing wooden clogs, in an attempt to get landowners to treat them fairly. Sometimes the crop circles were linked with witchcraft, and the people said to have made them suffered punishment for being witches. A woodcut print from an English political leaflet, dated 1678, depicted an image of a devil mowing grain in an oval-shaped pattern, in response to a rich landowner's statement that he'd rather pay the devil to work his fields than offer the reapers a higher wage. According to the story, the following night the greedy landowner found a circle made of flattened grain in his field.

Crop circle researchers suggest that whoever is responsible for making these forms may be trying to communicate with us, through the vehicle of symbol. If fairies do have a hand in the creation of crop circles, what message might they be attempting to send? Do they want to connect with us? Are they entreating us to behave more kindly toward the earth and all its inhabitants? Are they encouraging us to open our minds to receive knowledge from other realms of existence?

FAIRY RINGS

Peculiar circles of mushrooms that appear suddenly and unexpectedly, sometimes spreading for 100 feet or more, are known as fairy rings. The largest of these, found in Belfort, France, measured 2,000 feet in diameter and was estimated to be seven hundred years old. Today we understand these strange but natural occurrences to be the result of fungal growth, but our ancestors saw them as the work of the fae.

> "Few humans see fairies or hear their music, but many find fairy rings of dark grass, scattered with toadstools, left by their dancing feet."
>
> JUDY ALLEN, *Fantasy Encyclopedia*

In many parts of Western Europe and Britain, people believed that these rings resulted from fairies dancing in ritual circles that affected the grass, causing it to wither and leave room for mushrooms to sprout in its place. According to some tales, the rings marked the sites of underground fairy communities. Legends warned that the rings served as portals between earth and the fairy realm—anyone who stepped inside a fairy ring would be instantly swept away into the land of the fae. Other tales attributed the rings to witchcraft.

Witches Welcoming Spring

According to Germanic lore, witches—as well as fairies and other spirits—gathered in fairy rings on Walpurgisnacht (Beltane Eve, April 30) to welcome spring. Welsh stories say the mushrooms indicate places where hidden treasure lies beneath the forest floor. Austrian legends say the fiery breath of dragons scorches the earth, forming the mysterious rings.

LIMINAL ZONES

Because fairies travel regularly between their world and ours, they can sometimes be found in places where two realms come together and briefly merge. The slice of seacoast between low and high tides, the deepening foliage between field and forest, the sloping land between plain and mountain are a few of these in-between places. Known as liminal zones, these magickal spots aren't wholly one thing or the other—you can't determine precisely where one leaves off and the other begins. Consequently, they serve as bridges or portals that lead from one realm into another.

Dawn and dusk, too, can be considered liminal zones. At these transient times the interplay between nature's dualities is in evidence. Solar and lunar energies are shifting. A transfer of archetypal masculine and feminine power is taking place. During these fleeting moments, you're more likely to see fairies than at high noon when these sensitive beings recoil from harsh sunlight.

In these transitional spaces, you may notice your own boundaries softening, your definitions of what *is* and *isn't* blurring. Your sixth sense may become more acute, your second sight sharper. A previously undiscovered level of existence may open to you. Witness it with awe, reverence, and discernment.

> "If we opened our minds to enjoyment, we might find tranquil pleasures spread about us on every side. We might live with the angels that visit us on every sunbeam, and sit with the fairies who wait on every flower."
>
> SAMUEL SMILES, author

MUSICAL EVENTS

Fairies adore music and dancing, and they're experts in both areas. People who claim to have seen fairies often describe them as dancing in forest groves, in pastures blossoming with flowers, and at ancient stone monuments such as Stonehenge. The Russian rusalki are such energetic dancers that they exhaust their mortal partners, sometimes to the point of death.

The Nutcracker

"Dance of the Sugar Plum Fairy" from *The Nutcracker*, with music composed by Russia's Pyotr Ilyich Tchaikovsky and choreographed by Lev Ivanov, was first performed in 1892. It remains to this day one of the most beloved and enduring of all ballets. The elaborate production has been an annual tradition for the New York City Ballet since 1954.

You can be sure to find fairies in the audience at concerts and other musical events, even at pubs and street jams, especially when the performers play Celtic folk tunes. Scottish fairies like bagpipes. Eastern European fairies enjoy polkas. Legends say fairies have a fondness for flute music—whenever Mozart's fairy tale opera *The Magic Flute* is performed, it's safe to say that the fae are in attendance. Don't look for fairies at heavy metal and rap venues, however—the high decibel levels are too harsh for fairies' delicate ears.

Fairy Investigators

Founded in Britain in 1927, the Fairy Investigation Society gathers information about fairies and evidence of their existence. One of its founders, Barnard Sleigh, wrote about fairy sightings and interactions with human beings in his 1926 book *The Gates of the Horn Being Sundry Records from the Proceedings of the Society for the Investigation of Faery Fact & Fallacy*. He described the fae as spirit guardians of nature. The society, which once counted Walt Disney among its members, attempted to make contact with fairies, compiled accounts of fairy encounters, published a newsletter, and held meetings to share knowledge about the fae folk. In the 1990s, the society ceased operation, but in 2014 folklore historian Simon Young and his associates relaunched it online as *Fairyist*. You can visit their website Fairyist.com for all sorts of information about fairies, including sightings, books, artwork, movies, and fairy tales—you can even participate in a fairy census and share your personal stories about the fae.

THE THREE WORLDS OF CELTIC MYTH

Celtic myths refer to the realm beyond our own as the Otherworld. According to noted author Caitlin Matthews, in her book *The Celtic Book of the Dead*, "The Celtic Otherworld was believed to have a reality contiguous to and sometimes overlapping ordinary reality. The Celts had no heaven or hell. The Otherworld, like their philosophy, was non-dual in character. In theory, anyone could reach the Otherworld....The Celtic Otherworld is a mirror of this world, so our individual experience of the realm beyond death is influenced by our actions in this life."

Some sources tell us this is where the fae folk live. According to Irish legends, the Tuatha dé Danann, having departed the earthly realm, now dwell in the Otherworld. Other researchers, however, including Scottish author R.J. Stewart, say the fairy world is within what's known as the Underworld. In his book *Earth Light*, Stewart describes the fairy realm as "the Primal Land: wherever you are, whatever land you are in, the faery realm is the primal image of that land. It is before and beyond corruption and pollution...the faery realm *mirrors* our own...our world is devolved or reflected *out of* the primal image of the faery world."

Visits to Fairyland

In the late seventeenth century, Gaelic scholar and Scottish minister Robert Kirk studied the reports of Gaelic people who claimed to have seen and communicated with fairies. According to Reverend Kirk in his book *The Secret Commonwealth of Elves, Fauns, and Fairies*, some people also described physically moving into and out of the Underworld. In the fairies' land, these individuals said they saw the fae, ancestral spirits, and human beings who had been taken into the realm of the fairies.

Celtic mythology discusses three main "worlds" (although there are other planes of existence too). Kisma K. Stepanich, in her book *Faery Wicca Tarot*, calls these the Otherworld or Heavenly Realm, which is above our earthly one; the Plains, meaning our planet; and the Underworld, the primal land of which earth is a reflection. Maya Magee Sutton and Nicholas R. Mann, in *Druid Magic*, call the three worlds the Land of the Living, an infinite realm that contains the others and is where the soul or eternal Self resides when not embodied; the Fairy Realm, which is home to the fairies, gods and goddesses, and ancestors; and the Human World, where we live while incarnated. In the nineteenth century, Scottish folklorist and minister John Gregorson Campbell wrote about three Otherworlds, one inhabited by fairies, another by spirits including ghosts, and a third that he described as a world of good and evil where witches resided. Campbell's ideas are included in *The Gaelic Otherworld*, revised by Gaelic scholar Ronald Black. You'll find other explanations and descriptions of these worlds as well.

Yes, I admit, it's a little confusing. Here's my own interpretation, and I'm intentionally oversimplifying because, although there's a lot more to it, exploring this subject deeply is better left for another book.

- The Celts' Otherworld is what people who've undergone near-death experiences describe as "home," the place our souls occupy when they're not on earth (or someplace else).

- The Underworld is a place of primal power, the source from which manifest realms evolve, the etheric blueprint for our planet (and perhaps other planets and places as well).

- In between is Planet Earth, the physical world humans and other creatures occupy.

If you decide you want to visit these other levels of existence, I've suggested in Part Two a few techniques to help you enter and explore them.

THE WORLD TREE

Celtic mythology tells us the three worlds of existence are connected by a magnificent tree, known as the World Tree. Its branches reach into the Otherworld, its roots sink deep into the Underworld, and on its trunk nestles the earth plane.

Trees play roles as wisdom keepers and magickal entities in the myths and legends of many cultures. The Norse god Odin hung from the great tree Yggdrasil for nine days and nights, in order to bring the knowledge of the runes to humankind. The Tree of Knowledge is central to the Genesis story. In the Kabbalah, the Tree of Life provides a spiritual path to Divine Wisdom. The ancient Greeks believed every tree was embodied by a fairy called a dryad, who animated it and served as its enlivening spirit. Chinese myths speak of the goddess Wangmu Niangniang, in whose garden grew an exquisite peach tree that bore fruit only once every three thousand years; anyone who ate its peaches achieved immortality. The magickal Isle of Avalon in the Arthurian legends is said to be a paradise where apple trees grow profusely. Many Wiccans consider trees sacred—especially the birch, rowan, ash, alder, willow, hawthorn, oak, holly, and hazel—and burn a combination of these woods in ritual fires.

The Tree of Wisdom

According to one legend, the hazel tree stands at the center of the Otherworld. It is associated with justice and wisdom, as well as good fortune. Another legend says nine hazel trees surround the Well of Wisdom in the courtyard of the castle where Manannan mac Lir, the King of the Fairies, lives. Nuts from the trees fall into the well and are eaten by salmon—the Celtic fish that symbolizes knowledge. Whoever eats the salmon or the nuts gains magickal insight.

The Druids considered all trees to be sacred, and each tree had its own significance, qualities, correspondences, and powers. Usually, Druid rites and ceremonies were performed outdoors in groves of trees. Wiccans, too, are familiar with the magick and wisdom embodied by trees. We associate oaks with strength and longevity, and burn the wood of the mighty oak in our Yule fires. We value ash and rowan trees for their powers of protection. We use willows for dowsing and for enhancing intuition. Apple trees signify spiritual courage and can lead us into the Otherworld. According to myth, the Fairy Queen gave apples to mortals she favored that would allow them to access the land of the fae.

> "Collectively in the Celtic tradition, the trees form the World Tree. If we imagine all the species of trees and the aspects of existence they represent arranged in a circle, then at the center where all their qualities converge is the World Tree. This is the *axis mundi*, the axis that runs through the center of the Upper, Middle, and Lower Worlds, or, in the Celtic cosmology, sky, earth, and sea. As the World Tree is composed of all the trees in existence, it is therefore the source of all knowledge....Access to all the realms of Otherworlds is through the roots and branches of the World Tree."
>
> **MAYA MAGEE SUTTON and NICHOLAS R. MANN,** *Druid Magic*

Shamans frequently journey to other realms of existence—known as walking between the worlds—by traveling through a tree trunk, in some cases the trunk of the World Tree. Perhaps that's what the Buddha did when he sat beneath the Bodhi tree and gained enlightenment. You, too, can move gracefully through a majestic tree to access other levels of reality and to learn the secrets the old trees know—in Chapter 11 you'll find a technique that describes how to do this.

THE OGHAM ALPHABET

The Irish alphabet called Ogham is based on trees—the letters even look like stylized trees, with a central stave or trunk and lines branching off it. Each Ogham letter relates to a specific tree and has a distinctive meaning. For example, we associate oak trees with strength and endurance, and those are the qualities inherent in Ogham's letter *duir.* The berries of the yew are toxic, hence its letter *idho* represents death and transformation. Different versions of the alphabet evolved over time; the most common one is the Beth-Luis-Nion (named for the first three letters).

Ogham letters can be strung together to create words or phrases. The Celts carved Ogham script on standing stones throughout Britain and Ireland to mark graves, define property boundaries, and provide directions for travelers. Approximately four hundred of these inscribed stones still exist. Some sources say the tree alphabet was developed about fifteen hundred years ago, as a written form of the Irish language. Others suggest its creators may have intended it as a secret language that ordinary people and the Romans, in particular, couldn't understand. This tree alphabet does not appear to be related to any other language or form of writing.

> "Under the Celtic system, everything is believed to exist on three levels—physical, mental, and spiritual. In the case of Ogham, the physical level is the ink on the page or the notch on the stone, the mental is the word or letter that ink or notch makes you think of, and the spiritual level is all the associations that letter or word has when used as part of a system of spiritual development."
>
> STEVE BLAMIRES, *Celtic Tree Mysteries: Practical Druid Magic & Divination*

You can sign Ogham as well as write it, and in this it may be unique. Consider your torso, arm, or leg as the "trunk" of the tree, then position your fingers on either side of the center to form the "branches." In this way, you depict the letters corporeally.

In addition to having practical purposes, Ogham runes can be used for divination, just like the Norse runes. You can do readings with them, in the same way you might do tarot readings, by drawing certain runes and laying them out in patterns called spreads. Each letter and each position in the spread has a specific meaning. You can also engage the runes' magickal properties by wearing one or more of them, adding them to talismans and amulets, rendering them on ritual tools—in any way that you might use other magick symbols. I include them in some of my paintings when I'm creating visual spells and meditative aids. The cards in the *Faery Wicca Tarot* deck include Ogham letters in their symbolism. In Part Two, you'll find suggestions for bringing these ancient letters and the wisdom of trees into spellwork. Might the magickal power of trees be due, at least in part, to the presence of fairies living there? You can purchase Ogham runes online or make your own from wood, stone, ceramic, or metal.

Witchwood

Elder is also known as witchwood. Supposedly, bad luck will fall upon anyone who does not ask the tree's permission three times before harvesting any part of it—that's good advice when you're cutting any tree, not just elder. Folklore associates the elder with the crone aspect of the Goddess and with witches, thus elder wood is rarely used to make furniture or as firewood for fear of incurring their wrath. Rowan is also sometimes referred to as witchwood.

HOW TO RECOGNIZE A FAIRY'S PRESENCE

For centuries, people around the world have observed fairies and described their experiences with the fae folk. According to the twelfth-century *Colloquy of the Ancients*, even Saint Patrick supposedly encountered a beautiful young fairy woman in County Roscommon, Ireland. The fairy, a member of the Tuatha dé Danann, reportedly wore a green cloak and a golden crown. It's possible that fairies showed themselves more frequently to humans in earlier times, when people lived closer to nature, than they do now—and when people believed in fairies.

> "The fairies went from the world, dear
> Because men's hearts grew cold:
> And only the eyes of children see
> What is hidden from the old."
>
> **KATHLEEN FOYLE, poet**

Although you may never actually see a fully formed fairy, you can detect the presence of these spirits in other ways. People often describe seeing unusual lights, such as tiny twinkling sparks similar to fireflies or greenish glowing orbs. On a few occasions, I've witnessed fuzzy grayish balls about the size of a basketball zipping through my house—my cat saw one of them too, and chased after it.

You might hear faint music playing or the sound of tinkling bells. Or, you might smell a lovely floral aroma. Try to identify the scent, and then look up the meaning of that particular flower—it may be a fairy message that has a special significance for you. While writing this book, I repeatedly smelled pipe smoke and wondered if a leprechaun might be nearby. Some people sense a sudden, inexplicable shift in the temperature of a room or a light breeze blowing even though the windows are shut.

> "You know how sometimes, you catch the faintest hint of movement in the corner of your eye, then you blink and it's gone? That's them."
>
> JENNIFER MCMAHON, *Don't Breathe a Word*

If you're outdoors, you might spot movement in the grass, even though nothing physical seems to cause the movement. Or, you may notice a place where the grass has been flattened in a circular pattern—perhaps even two or more interlocking circles. "Faces" glimpsed in the bark of a tree trunk or in its leaves could indicate the presence of a fairy. If you gaze into a pond and see flattish bubbles form on the surface, you might be looking at water spirits known as undines.

Greet the fairies with respect. Listen carefully in case they want to impart information to you. Remember, though, you can't command a fairy's presence. The fae will only let you witness them if they choose.

BEST TIMES TO CONNECT WITH FAIRIES

As mentioned earlier, dawn and dusk are good times to connect with fairies. Some sources say fairies prefer nighttime to daylight, and they're especially active at midnight. According to an old pagan belief, the time between midnight and 3:00 a.m. on the night of the full moon is called the "Witching Hour." During this brief period, the spirit world and earth are closer than at other times of the month, allowing fairies to interact with us more easily, although we often consider their visitations to be dreams or fantasies.

The high energy on the Wiccan sabbats—Samhain, Yule, Imbolc, Ostara, Beltane, Midsummer, Lughnasadh, and Mabon—can also encourage closer alignment between humans and the fae, in part because these holidays mark the changing relationships between the sun and earth, which cause the seasons and make us aware of our connection with nature. On Samhain, the most sacred of Wiccan holidays, the veil between the seen and unseen worlds is thinnest. Therefore you're more likely to get a peek into the land of the fae on the night of October 31 than at other times of the year.

Fairy Holidays

If you hope to meet fairies from a particular country or culture, find out what dates or periods are special to them. For example, if you'd like to witness Persian peris, the Rose Water Festival, held between April 21 and May 21, is an ideal time. During this time, the city of Kashan, Iran, considered the birthplace of roses, is radiant with the colors and scents of roses—and the presence of beautiful peris.

Like us, fairies have favorite places. If you see one in a certain spot, there's a good chance you'll see it there again. That odd-looking mound or grove of trees may be a fairy meeting place. Perhaps it's the site of a fae community or a doorway into their world. Be persistent. Visit the site regularly. Once the fairies get accustomed to seeing you around, they may relax their guard and reveal themselves to you. Bring gifts of food and drink to entice the fae.

Fairies and Countries

In case you're wondering, you can meet a fairy that's usually associated with Ireland, such as a leprechaun, in Australia or Poland or Korea—they don't show up only in the folklore of those countries. Sometimes we notice a particular type of fairy appearing in more than one country or culture; for example, Britain's brownies are similar to Germany's kobolds. You can also work with a water fairy, such as a merrow, even if you live in the high desert of Marfa, Texas. That's because fairies don't have physical bodies. Unlike us, they can go anywhere they please. You're more likely to find a woodland fairy in the forest than a desert, but when you're dealing with the fae, anything's possible.

As with all relationships, fairy-human associations take time to develop and require careful tending. The more energy you invest, the more likely you are to receive fairy assistance in return. In the next chapter we'll consider ways to win the fairies' favor and bring them into your magickal practice.

Chapter 5

INVITE FAIRIES TO ASSIST IN YOUR MAGICKAL WORK

Before you actually invite fairies to become your magickal coworkers, consider what you hope to gain from a collaboration with them—just as you would if you were forming a cooperative venture with human beings. What assets do certain fairies have that can benefit you? What can you learn from them? What do you hope to accomplish through this partnership? You might want to make a list of your objectives and review it periodically, as your intentions may change over time.

In this chapter we'll consider the advantages of partnering with the fae in your magickal practice. You'll also learn ways to attract fairies and convince them to assist you. I'll share tips and techniques for working with fairies; suggestions for winning their favor; and ways you can incorporate crystals, herbs, and other tools you use regularly in spells and rituals into your work with fairies.

BENEFITS OF WORKING WITH THE FAE

Fairies possess many abilities and talents that most humans lack, as we discussed in Chapter 1. If they agree to assist you, they can teach you some of their skills, including the following:

- **HEALING**—Fairies are well known for their healing abilities. They can expand your knowledge of herbal medicine in particular. In addition, they can help you manipulate the energetic forces in our universe to nurture yourself and others.

- **SHAPESHIFTING**—No, the fairies won't literally change you into a cat or a horse or an eagle. But they can show you how to tap in to the attributes of various creatures—a cat's grace, a horse's speed, an eagle's vision—and use these qualities to your advantage.

- **INTUITION**—Everyone has psychic ability, but most of us don't develop it fully. Fairies can teach you to strengthen your intuition and use it in ways you may not have done before, such as to divine the future.

- **HAPPINESS**—In general, fairies enjoy life more than a lot of humans do. That's partly because they don't regret the past or worry about the future. They don't try to live up to the expectations of others or indulge in self-criticism. By dancing and singing with the fae, you can achieve a greater sense of levity and acceptance.

- **EXPANDED CONSCIOUSNESS**—As discussed in Chapter 4, fairies move easily between the various worlds. They can serve as your guides—what the seventeenth-century Scottish minister, fairy researcher, and Gaelic scholar Robert Kirk called "co-walkers"—and show you places you never imagined existed.

Bringing fairy energy into your spells and rituals can also add octane. Because many of the fae serve as guardians and caretakers of the natural world, they know the best ways to work with the energies of plants and stones. They understand the elements, solar and lunar cycles, and weather patterns. If you win their favor, they'll share their secrets with you.

KEEP A BOOK OF SHADOWS

If you're like many witches, you probably keep a very special type of journal known as a book of shadows or grimoire. This journal is more than a diary of what's going on in your daily life—it's an intimate account of your spiritual journey, the steps you take on the road to self-discovery, and what you learn along the way about the Craft of the Wise.

Here you pen information about your practice as a witch, the spells and rituals you perform, and your ongoing exploration of the mysteries that lie beyond the ordinary mundane world. Between your book's covers you also reveal your soul's secrets, as well as your expressions in the outer world—particularly those of a magickal and spiritual nature.

You may want to create a separate book of shadows in which to record your experiences with the fae. Which fairies did you collaborate with? Where did you meet them? What transpired during your relations with the fae? What challenges did you encounter and how did you handle them? What successes or failures did you have? In addition to writing down the spells you perform, discuss your feelings, insights, visions, dreams, meditations, and musings.

Be sure to note the dates and times of your interactions with the fairies. You may also want to include data about moon phases, astrological information, weather conditions, and situations in your everyday life that might have influenced your experiences.

BRINGING FAIRIES INTO YOUR PRACTICE

Now that you've decided to bring the fae into your magickal practice, you're ready to take the first steps to establishing a good working relationship with them. In Chapter 2, we discussed some of the fairies and how they can assist you. Determine which ones have the skills, proclivities, and temperaments to partner with you. If none of these fae folk seems to fit the bill, do some additional research. For instance, if you're looking for an edge in an athletic competition, you might petition the Norse Valkyries, who decide which warriors will win a battle. My book *Fairies: The Myths, Legends, & Lore* discusses fairies from many cultures around the world.

You may seek a single interaction with a fairy for a specific purpose. Or, you may choose to establish an ongoing relationship with one or more of the fae. Either way, it's wise to proceed slowly and cautiously. For the most part, fairies are wary of humans and don't really like us very much. That's not surprising, given all the damage we've wreaked on Planet Earth and its animal inhabitants, and the way our pop culture has demeaned the fairies. Plus, they consider themselves a superior race—in some cases, the perfect prototypes from which we evolved—so you'll have to make it worth their while to associate with you.

Let's say you've decided to invite a household fairy, such as a brownie or kobold, into your home to help out with domestic chores. Start by setting offerings of food and drink outside your home, on the porch or patio. Gradually move the gifts inside, leaving them by the doorway, and finally into the area of your home where you'd like the fairies to pitch in.

From Servant to Celebrity

In J.M. Barrie's original story *Peter Pan*, Tinker Bell was a common kitchen fairy before she evolved into an international celebrity. A tinker is someone who mends pots, pans, and other household items, and in her early days—before she had a theme park of her own—Tink lived in a teapot.

Consider writing a letter to the fairies with whom you'd like to work. If you're interested in interacting with a Celtic fairy, write in Ogham. If you think the Norse fairies might be better partners for you, write in Norse runes. (Naturally, they'll understand your native tongue too—they communicate telepathically anyway.) Explain your intentions as simply as possible—you might only need to use a single glyph to get your point across. For example, if your objective is to enhance your strength, endurance, or personal power, draw the Ogham glyph *duir* (the Irish word for "oak") on a piece of paper. Fold the paper around a piece of honey cake (or another treat) and place it in an oak tree for the fairies to find.

FAIRY DOORS

If you've ever gone on a shamanic journey, you may be familiar with the practice of mentally entering a narrow opening into a secret cave or burrowing into the roots of an ancient tree whose trunk connects this world to one beyond. (Chapter 11 provides information about how to do this.) Like these portals, fairy doors serve as passageways between earth and the magickal land of the fae. A knot in a gnarled old oak or a uniquely shaped gap in a stone wall could be a fairy door—if you peek through it, you just might glimpse a world you never realized existed.

If you want fairies to visit you, you may want to install a modern-day "fairy door" in your home or yard to grant access to the fae. Usually, these entryways are small—about the size of a cat door—based on the misconception that all fairies are diminutive. Of course, fairies can change shape at will, so if they decide to enter your environment they can shrink to whatever size they need to be to get in.

Position the door in a remote spot, away from traffic and human activity— and where your dog won't chase them. Decorate it with colorful ribbons, shiny beads, feathers, shells, coins, and other trinkets to attract the fairies. Leave offerings of food and drink there too.

Before you install a fairy door, however, give some thought to why you want to invite the fae into your home. Remember, not all fairies are benevolent—some can be real nuisances. You probably don't want to put the welcome mat out to all these spirits. Think of yourself as a landlord—what sort of tenants are you seeking? Which fairies do you want to associate with? How do you plan to work with them? What are your objectives and expectations? Before you put out a "vacancy" sign, learn all you can about the fairies you think will get along best with you and the other occupants of your home.

CREATE A FAIRY GARDEN

Nature fairies, as you might expect, enjoy hanging out in gardens. Your fairy garden can be as lavish or as simple as you want it to be. If you have a large yard, you might want to plant flowers, shrubs, maybe a vegetable or herb garden—you can use the flowers and herbs in your spells too. This is the ideal spot for a fairy altar, which I discuss in the following section. Here are a few other suggestions:

- Put a birdbath or fountain in your garden. Water fairies such as the undines and nymphs will love it—so will the birds, butterflies, and other creatures.

- Hang tiny bells or a wind chime in your garden—the tinkling sound will appeal to music-loving fairies.

- Bright, shiny objects attract fairies, so consider hanging crystal pendants from tree branches. Or, put colored glass gazing balls in your garden. Christmas tree ornaments that don't have religious pictures on them will delight the fairies too.

- Remove anything made of iron—folklore says iron repels fairies.

- Don't insult the fairies by plunking down tacky garden statues of gnomes, leprechauns, or other fae folk.

- Use only organic fertilizers and pest repellants in your fairy garden.

> "Faeries are known to be tenders of plants and energizing inhabitants of gardens. They are more elusive than Angels and often have lively, mercurial temperaments. They are active in preserving what little wilderness remains on the Earth."
>
> ELIZABETH EILER, *Swift and Brave: Sacred Souls of Animals*

Those of you who live in city apartments can plant fairy gardens on a smaller scale, using containers, window boxes, or a few house plants. Some cities have community gardens where you might establish a small plot, thereby inviting fairies to come to an urban area they might ordinarily avoid. Even a city park can serve as a fairy garden. By visiting it regularly, leaving offerings for the fae, and sending them messages—intuitively or otherwise—that convey your intentions, you let the fairies know you seek to form a closer relationship with them. The more you think about them and demonstrate your interest in meeting them, the more often you'll get a peek at the fae folk.

FAIRY ALTARS

An altar is a witch's "workbench," a place to cast spells, display ritual tools, interact with spirits, meditate—whatever you do in your magickal practice. You may already have an altar in your home or in an outdoor spot that's sacred to you. Some witches erect altars or shrines to favorite deities they honor. Some position four altars at the four directions. Others set up temporary altars for specific reasons.

Where Should You Place a Fairy Altar?

A fairy altar serves two purposes: to attract one or more fairies, and to establish a place to work with the fae. Ideally, the altar should be located outdoors, in a safe and secluded spot away from human activity, vehicular traffic, and buildings. Craft it of materials you've found in nature; for example, lay a flat stone atop two other stones. An interesting tree stump or a fallen log might make a good fairy altar too.

In a yard or garden, you could repurpose a birdbath, a stone garden bench, or a wooden picnic table into a fairy altar. If you must create the altar inside your home, or if you've decided you want to attract household fairies, you can use a table or a shelf. Depending on your living arrangements, you may choose to make a temporary altar from a box that your housemates won't identify as anything out of the ordinary, and in which you can store items you'll use in your work with the fae.

What Should You Put on the Altar?

Place offerings for the fairies on the altar. Although most fairies enjoy milk, honey, sweets, and bread, they have their individual tastes, just like we do. Leprechauns prefer ale and tobacco. Undines are fond of perfume and essential oils. Fire spirits are drawn to candles. Incense is a good gift for sylphs. Curious creatures, fairies are intrigued by things they wouldn't ordinarily find in their native environments. For instance, seashells might fascinate forest fairies. Lava rocks might captivate Cornish fairies. Here are some other suggestions:

- Keep the altar as well as the area around it neat and clean—most fairies appreciate tidiness.

- Decorate it in accordance with the changing seasons, with daffodils in springtime, pine cones in winter, and so on.

- Program a crystal with your intention and set it on the altar. Unless you intend the crystal as a gift for the fairies, don't leave it there unattended, or chances are they'll appropriate it.

Choose organic food and beverages as offerings for the fairies—they'll recoil from pesticides and genetically modified edibles. If your fairy altar is located outdoors, decorate it with natural, biodegradable materials—avoid plastics and synthetic fabrics. By showing respect for nature, you also show respect for the fairies who protect it.

PLAY MUSIC AND DANCE

No fairy gathering would be complete without music and dancing. The folklore and fairy tales of myriad cultures describe the fae engaged in this favorite form of entertainment, whether they're celebrating a special holiday or just spinning about in a sunlit meadow for the sheer joy of it. Many people who claim to have seen fairies describe watching them dance in a circle. It's said that the fairies meet in the woods at midnight, where they dance and sing as they perform their magick—leaving behind the fairy rings we discussed in Chapter 4. According to Irish legend, people who've spent time in fairyland and heard fairy music, known as *Ceol-Sidhe*, are never the same again—a wistful, distant look glazes their eyes, and the sound of a fairy harp fills their ears.

The noted Russian composer Pyotr Ilyich Tchaikovsky wrote his ballet *The Sleeping Beauty* based on the fairy tale. It was first performed in 1890 and is considered one of his finest works. Shakespeare made fairy music and dancing a prominent part of his delightful play *A Midsummer Night's Dream.*

"Oberon: 'Through the house give glimmering light,
By the dead and drowsy fire:
Every elf and fairy sprite
Hop as light as bird from brier;
And this ditty, after me,
Sing, and dance it trippingly.'
Titania: 'First, rehearse your song by rote
To each word a warbling note:
Hand in hand, with fairy grace,
Will we sing, and bless this place.'"

WILLIAM SHAKESPEARE, *A Midsummer Night's Dream*

What instruments and tunes do fairies favor? Leprechauns reportedly play tin whistles, fiddles, and harps. Disney's fairies blow shell horns and flower trumpets. Human musicians today play fairy music on zithers, Aeolian flutes, piccolos, bagpipes, celestas, bells, and drums such as the bodhran, as well as fiddles and harps.

What Does Fairy Music Sound Like?

In 1921, professional musician Thomas Wood claimed he heard fairy music, describing it as "essentially harmonic. It was not a melody, an 'air.' It sounded like the weaving together of various tenuous fairy strands.' When he was later told that Irish fairy music was 'a waving in the air' he agreed enthusiastically. Forty years later, in the same place, he once again heard the mesmerizing fairy music, which he said was 'like glass bells—very, very beautiful.'" The Fairy Investigation Society's website Fairyist.com displays written examples of fairy music.

If you're a musician, bring your instrument(s) to the altar and play. Invite the fae to join you for a jam. Otherwise, play music on your phone or another device. Celtic tunes, peaceful instrumental pieces, and classical music are good choices. Loud, harsh, or percussive synthesized music will probably scare away the fairies—their sensitive hearing can't bear the noise of heavy metal or rap. Legends say the fae don't like the sound of church bells, so skip the religious songs too.

MAGICK TOOLS

Witches and magick workers of other traditions generally use a variety of tools in their practice. Although technically you don't need any physical equipment, the tools improve your focus and help shift your thinking from mundane to magickal. You may already own the four principal tools: wand, pentagram, chalice, and athame. Quite likely, you also use crystals and gemstones, candles, incense, and herbs. Perhaps you work with a cauldron, besom, bells, essential oils, cords, oracles, a scrying mirror, and other implements as well.

Fairy tales and folklore tell us the fae also use magick tools. As mentioned in Chapter 2, the Tuatha dé Danann possessed four powerful tools that bear similarities to the major ones witches prize—perhaps they inspired the tools we use today.

Wands, Spears, and Staves

The Danann's spear of the god Lugh, which always struck its mark, corresponds to the witch's wand. In some tarot decks, the suit of Wands is depicted as the suit of Spears. Both tools symbolize the fire element. Today, of course, we don't wield a spear, stave, or wand as a weapon; its purpose is to direct energy. Stories frequently describe fairies waving magick wands—think of the fairy godmother in "Cinderella," who used hers to transform a pumpkin into a coach and mice into horses. The leprechaun's shillelagh also resembles a wand. If you join forces with the fairies, they may teach you new ways to use your own wand.

Chalices and Cauldrons

The Danann's cauldron of the god Dagda, which was never empty and always provided food for all, symbolizes the element of water, as does the chalice. Legends and lore depict fairies and witches with both tools. Perhaps the best-known example appears in Shakespeare's *Macbeth* in which three witches stir a magick brew in a cauldron while chanting "Double, double, toil and trouble." The Irish goddess Brigid, whose sabbat Wiccans celebrate on Imbolc, is usually shown with a cauldron (see Chapter 12). And of course, the most famous chalice of all is the Holy Grail, which some people say now lies at the bottom of the Chalice Well in Glastonbury, England. In Part Two you'll find suggestions for using both cauldrons and chalices in spellcraft.

Sword of Nuada

The Danann's sword of Nuada, god of the hunt, brought victory in battle. It corresponds to the witch's athame or ritual dagger and symbolizes the element of air. Modern-day witches don't fight battles with swords or athames, however. In fact, we now believe an athame should never have drawn blood. We use these tools to disperse energy, cut through psychic obstacles, and sever bonds. You can also use either tool to cast a circle. The most famous sword in mythology is King Arthur's Excalibur, immortalized in Sir Thomas Malory's fifteenth-century version of the legend, *Le Morte d'Arthur*. Upon Arthur's death, the great sword was returned to its source, the Lady of the Lake, who may have been a Celtic lake fairy like the Welsh *gwragged annwn*.

Stone of Destiny

The Danann's stone of destiny, called Lia Fail, connected them to the land and enabled them to choose Ireland's human kings and queens. It symbolizes the element of earth, as does the witch's pentagram. Magick stones show up frequently in mythology, one of the best-known being the Philosopher's Stone, which had the power to transform lead into gold. Crystals and gemstones, too, embody the earth element. Fairy lore tells us the fae imbued crystals and gemstones with ancient wisdom, giving them the power to work healing magick.

Program a Crystal

Crystals are sensitive, intelligent life-forms capable of holding, amplifying, and projecting your intentions. The various shapes, colors, inclusions, and so on influence the crystals' powers and uses. You can place an intention in a crystal, thereby "programming" it to assist you in spellwork.

1. First, cleanse the crystal with mild soap and water.
2. Next, envision pure white light surrounding and permeating the crystal, clearing it of any unwanted energies that might interfere with your spell.
3. Hold the crystal to your third eye on your forehead between your eyebrows. Visualize the outcome you desire and imagine sending the intention into the crystal. The image will remain there until you remove it.
4. Hold the crystal to your lips and tell it what you'd like it to do.

Your crystal is now ready to assist you. Treat all crystals and gemstones with respect, and they'll serve you well. Many witches wear quartz crystals for protection. If you decide to wear one as a pendant, don't drill holes in it you'll kill it. Instead, wrap it with jeweler's wire. In Part Two you'll find numerous techniques for working with crystals in spellcraft.

MAGICKAL BOTANICALS

Most witches do some type of plant magick—that may be true for you too. Herbs and other botanicals give us their physical substance for healing, food, scent, and other practical purposes, as well as their energetic properties for spellcraft. These versatile life-forms are probably the most frequently used ingredients in magick. As we've already discussed, the nature fairies care for flowers, trees, herbs, and other plants on earth, so anytime you work with botanicals you're working with the fae.

Each plant has its unique characteristics and powers. Roses, for instance, are favorites for love spells. Basil is a popular herb for protection spells. Mint attracts prosperity. For your convenience, the Appendix at the back of this book lists some herbs and their characteristics, but other authors have written more comprehensive texts devoted solely to the practice of botanical magick and green witchcraft.

Tips for Working with Plants

Yes, there is such a thing as plant etiquette. Plants are sensitive, living things with feelings and souls. In *The Secret Life of Plants*, authors Peter Tompkins and Christopher Bird write about the experiments of polygraph expert Cleve Backster, which demonstrated that plants are sentient beings with memory, communication abilities, and ESP—they even have preferences in music. Consider these guidelines when you're working with plants and the nature spirits that guard them.

- Always use wild or organically grown plants in magick work. Grow your own, if possible.

- Before cutting a plant (or part of it), ask its permission.

- Thank the plant for assisting you and leave a gift for it in return, perhaps a small crystal or a little wine.

- Fresh plants produce faster results; dried plant material has more enduring effects.

- Essential oils are more intense in their actions than fresh or dried flowers.

- Concoctions made from plant material, such as potions and lotions, will last longer if you store them in brown or green glass bottles in a cool place.

- Some plants are toxic. That doesn't mean you should avoid working with them, for they have definite value in spellcraft and can be quite powerful. Use caution and common sense, however.

Learn as much as you can about the plants you'll be working with, magickally or medicinally. Your health, well-being, and the success of your spells depend on your knowledge of the forces with which you're dealing.

Favorite Fairy Plants

Different people will tell you different things about which fairies like which plants best, and which botanicals should be used in fairy magick or planted in fairy gardens. Nature fairies, whose job it is to nurture and tend the plants on our planet, treasure all of them. Having said that, here are some theories espoused by other fairy enthusiasts.

- **MUSHROOMS:** Mushrooms, as we've already discussed, spring up mysteriously when fairies dance, creating "fairy rings." Diminutive fairies are said to use mushrooms as tables and stools.

- **FERNS:** Supposedly, pixies are fond of ferns. Legends say fern seeds collected on Midsummer's Eve can be used in spells for invisibility (see Chapter 12).

- **PRIMROSES:** According to folklore, primroses have the power to open doorways into fairyland.

- **ST. JOHN'S WORT:** Legends say this plant is anathema to fairies. Therefore, it's a popular herb for protection against the fae.

- **FOXGLOVE:** In Britain this flower is called "elf's glove" and "fairy cap." Tiny fairies wear the blossoms of this toxic (to humans, cats, and dogs) flowering plant as pretty hats.

- **COWSLIPS:** Another name for this flower is "fairy cup." Folklore says they mark the site of fairy gold. Shakespeare mentions cowslips several times in his plays; in *The Tempest* the fairy Ariel lies in a cowslip blossom.

- **LILIES:** In *A Midsummer's Night Dream* the Bard describes the Fairy King Oberon as carrying a lily wand.

- **PANSY:** Sometimes called "fairy face," the juice of these flowers was used by the fairy Puck in *A Midsummer's Night Dream* to make "man or woman madly dote upon the next live creature that it sees."

- **CLOVER:** Obviously, the lucky four-leaf clover is a favorite of leprechauns.

- **HOLLY:** Northern fairies are said to take shelter beneath holly bushes during the cold winter months.

> "[The children] made wreaths of flowers and hung them upon the tree and about the spring to please the fairies that lived there; for they liked that, being idle innocent little creatures, as all fairies are, and fond of anything delicate and pretty like wild flowers put together that way. In return for this attention the fairies did any friendly thing they could for the children, such as keeping the spring always full and clear and cold, and driving away serpents and insects that sting; and so there was never any unkindness between the fairies and the children during more than five hundred years."
>
> MARK TWAIN, *Joan of Arc*

Now it's time to begin doing magick with the fairies. In Part Two, you'll find a variety of spells, rituals, blessings, potions, talismans, meditations, and activities for a wide range of purposes. There's also a chapter of practices to perform on the Wiccan/pagan sabbats. Design your own spells too—the more personal and heartfelt a spell, the more powerful it is.

Always protect yourself before you begin a spell with the fairies. Chapter 8 includes some suggestions you may want to use for this purpose. And remember to record your experiences in your book of shadows.

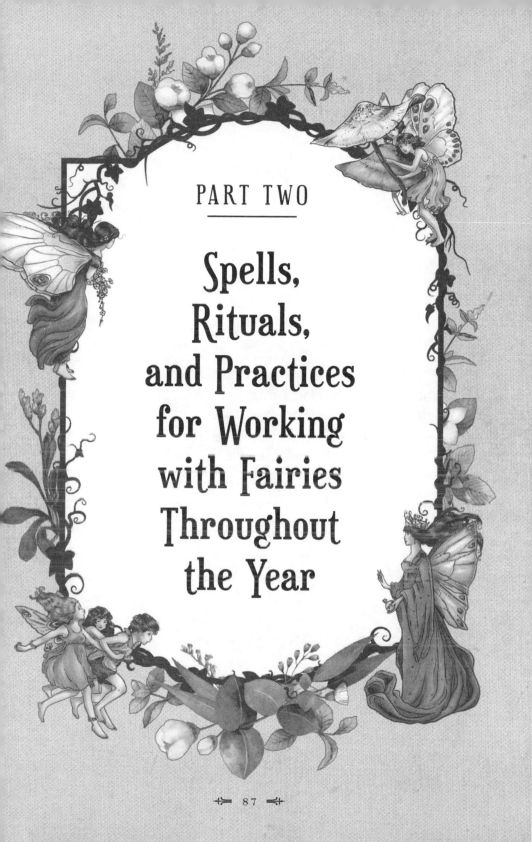

PART TWO

Spells, Rituals, and Practices for Working with Fairies Throughout the Year

Chapter 6

WORKING WITH FAIRIES FOR LOVE AND FRIENDSHIP

As Shakespeare wrote in his play *A Midsummer's Night Dream*, "The course of true love never did run smooth." Not surprisingly, witches cast more love spells than any other kind. Even non-witches perform love spells; they just don't realize it. Hanging mistletoe above a doorway, for example, is a favorite pagan love spell. Toasting a bride and groom's happiness has magickal roots, and dancing around a Maypole is an age-old fertility ritual.

Since ancient times, witches have done spells to attract a new lover, increase a partner's ardor, smooth the bumps in a relationship, or deter an unwanted suitor. We still do. When you invite fairies to participate in spells for love and friendship you up the ante, so to speak. Fairy magick can boost the intensity of a spell or ritual, but it can also increase the risks—witness the trickery, illusions, and complications in *A Midsummer Night's Dream*. Use extra care and caution when spellcasting with the fae. Remember, they don't feel emotions the way we do, nor do they subscribe to the same ethics as humans. Fairies express unconditional love instead of personal, romantic love as we know it.

GUIDING ROMANCE

Which fairies can guide you in relationships with romantic partners and friends? Which ones can help you heal from emotional disappointments or losses? Which can share the secrets of seduction with you or teach you how to attract people who are right for you?

- **UNDINES:** Spirits who inhabit the waterways of the world, undines can offer assistance in emotional areas. Working with them can improve your intuition and insight into matters involving relationships.

- **MERROWS:** The beautiful water spirits called merrows reportedly come ashore to meet and marry human men, according to Irish legends. They even raise interspecies children and are more sociable than many fairies. A merrow may also help you gain riches through partnerships.

- **KORRIGANS:** These seductive Breton fairies can show you how to enhance your attractiveness. They know the secrets of love and sex magick, but be careful dealing with them for they can be manipulative tricksters.

> "I met a lady in the meads,
> Full beautiful—a faery's child,
> Her hair was long, her foot was light,
> And her eyes were wild.
> I made a garland for her head,
> And bracelets too, and fragrant zone;
> She looked at me as she did love,
> And made sweet moan
> I set her on my pacing steed,
> And nothing else saw all day long,
> For sidelong would she bend, and sing
> A faery's song."
>
> **JOHN KEATS,** *La Belle Dame sans Merci*

MAGICK FLOWER WATER FOR SELF-LOVE

In the 1930s, English physician Edward Bach developed a holistic form of healing that used flowers to aid a variety of emotional conditions. His thirty-eight original remedies incorporated the vital energy or essences of flowers, infused in a water and brandy solution. Bach's remedies have proved effective in treating conditions such as stress, insomnia, impatience, and anxiety. Their healing power may be rooted in fairy wisdom and the influence of nature spirits in the plant world. Make this flower water to enhance your sense of self-love—if you love and accept yourself, other people will too.

You Will Need

- Edible flower blossoms
- 8 ounces of spring water, preferably collected from a stream, lake, or well that has special meaning for you (make sure the water is potable if you plan to drink it)
- A ritual bowl or chalice
- A green or brown glass jar or bottle (with no words or pictures on it)
- A small vial of perfume or essential oil

Directions

1. Select fresh flower blossoms (wild or organically grown) that resonate with loving energy, such as roses, violets, hibiscus, honeysuckle, or nasturtium. Caution: Some flowers are toxic, so make sure to choose edible flowers.

2. Pour the water into your bowl or chalice.

3. Invite a water fairy known as an undine to participate in the preparation of this magick water. Fairies don't experience self-doubt or self-criticism, so they can help you overcome those feelings in yourself. You may notice ripples, rainbows, or tiny bubbles developing in the water, a sign that the undine has agreed to assist you.

4. Float the blossoms in the water and set them in the sunshine for about an hour to infuse the water with their vitality.

5. When you sense the water is ready, remove the flowers. You can use them for other purposes, if you like, perhaps dry them for sachets or potpourri.

6. Wash the bottle, then pour the flower water into it.

7. Thank the undine for her assistance.

8. Pour the perfume or essential oil into a stream, river, lake, or other body of water, preferably the one from which you collected the water for this spell. This is your thank-you gift to the undine.

9. Drink 1 ounce of the flower water each day, for eight days. Store the magick water in your fridge.

GLAMOUR SPELL

The term "casting a glamour" refers to a type of illusion you create by manipulating the energy around you. In so doing, you alter the way people see you and thus make yourself more appealing. You don't actually change yourself physically; instead, you temporarily enhance your attractiveness with magick. It's more like putting on makeup than getting cosmetic surgery. Fairies are experts at this technique—they regularly use their skills to project whatever image they choose. Ask a merrow to show you her tricks, for a glamour really is a trick to fool the eye.

You Will Need
- A mirror, preferably a full-length one
- A piece of costume jewelry

Directions
1. Choose one of your physical features that you consider beautiful, such as your eyes, hair, or smile.

2. Stand in front of your mirror and focus your attention on this lovely feature.

3. Silence the inner critic. Don't allow your thoughts to stray to things you consider less than perfect.

4. Compliment yourself profusely—indulge your vanity. This isn't a time for modesty. Say aloud something like "I'M BEAUTIFUL" or "I HAVE A WONDERFUL FIGURE" or "I'M HOT."

5. Strike some alluring poses. Look at yourself from various angles. Don't be embarrassed—no one else is watching. Have fun. This is a type of make-believe, but it only works if you believe it yourself.

6. Continue telling yourself how desirable you are. Notice more things about yourself that are appealing. Allow your self-appreciation to spread until it includes your entire being.

7. Sense the energy around you glowing—you might even see your aura growing brighter. Reach out and grab handfuls of this energy. Rub the sparking energy around your body, massaging it into your aura as if you were rubbing lotion into your skin.

8. Do this for as long as you like, until you feel confident in your beauty. Because a glamour only lasts a short time, several hours or so, it's best to put it on right before you meet the person(s) you want to impress.

9. Leave the piece of jewelry on your altar (or another place where the merrow will find it) as a thank-you gift

CELTIC LOVER'S KNOT

For more than fifteen hundred years, Celtic people have created intricate, interwoven patterns known as Celtic knots (sometimes called mystic knots). These designs had symbolic meanings and decorated standing stones, monuments, documents, architecture, jewelry, tools, and more. Perhaps the most famous and exquisite example of manuscript illustration featuring Celtic knots is the *Book of Kells*, which dates to the eighth century C.E.

The Celtic love knot is one of many lover's knots. You can use it for this spell, or if you prefer, find another design you like better. You can even create your own. Invite an Irish merrow to enhance your spell with her magick.

> "Celtic knot work represents the Thread of Life. The human soul is thought to be a fragment of the Divine, which will ultimately return to its Divine Source....The interlaced, or latticed, knot work patterns, with their unbroken lines, symbolize the process of humankind's eternal Spiritual evolution."
>
> **KISMA K. STEPANICH**, *Faery Wicca Tarot*

You Will Need

- A piece of pink paper
- A felt-tip marker, pen, or pencil
- Rose, jasmine, ylang-ylang, or musk essential oil
- A silver heart-shaped charm

Directions

1. Before you begin, give some thought to what you hope to accomplish with this spell. What do you desire in this relationship? What do you bring to the partnership? If you intend to attract a new romantic partner, what qualities do you seek in this person? If you hope to enhance an existing relationship, what areas would you like to improve and what can you do to facilitate this?

2. On the piece of pink paper, draw the symbol of a Celtic love knot (or download the pattern from the Internet and print it).

3. Keep your mind focused on your intention as you work. Notice that the lines in this design entwine and are endless, symbolizing the enduring quality of the new love you seek to draw to you or of the existing relationship you want to strengthen.

4. After you've finished drawing the outlines of the knot, begin writing your intentions in the pathways of the design. State these as affirmations: short, positive statements written in the present tense, such as "I now have a partner who's right for me in every way." You can write single words, if you prefer, such as trust, kindness, strength, intelligence, affection, etc.

5. When you feel your design is complete, run your fingertip through the pathways and read aloud what you've written there.

6. Dab a drop of essential oil in each corner of the piece of paper, then say aloud: "So MOTE IT BE" to seal the spell.

7. Display the Celtic knot on your altar, in your bedroom, or another place where you'll see it often.

8. Leave the charm for the merrow as a thank-you gift.

TIE AN OLD-FASHIONED LOVER'S KNOT

In days of old, women tucked bits of their lover's hair into lockets for safekeeping. Because the locket hung near the woman's heart, it was in constant contact with her heart chakra and feelings for her beloved. Witches use hair in spellwork because it lasts practically forever and because it contains a person's DNA, etheric signature, and life energy. This spell hearkens back to earlier times, while offering a bit of romance and nostalgia for modern-day lovers. It requires careful attention and patience, as do all important relationships. A Celtic merrow or a korrigan may be willing to help you with this spell. Just remember that the korrigans are tricksters, so you'll need to exercise caution to avoid getting caught up in their own agendas.

You Will Need
- A single hair or lock of your hair
- A single hair or lock of your lover's hair
- Hair gel (optional)
- A locket (optional)
- A plant (optional)
- A piece of jewelry for the fairy who aids you and food/libation for the nature fairies

Directions
1. Tie together your hair and your lover's hair. Depending on your intention, tie two, three, six, or eight knots. (Using hair gel can make this process easier.) Two is the number of partnership; three signifies manifestation in the physical world; six celebrates joy, creativity, and romantic ideals; eight symbolizes permanence and stability.

2. As you tie each knot, state aloud your intention. What do you hope to attain, enhance, or secure in this partnership? Remember to state your intention in a positive way and in the present tense, as if the situation you desire already exists.

3. If you have a locket, you may choose to follow in the steps of our ancestors and fit the hair knot into the locket. Otherwise, you can set the lover's knot on your altar, nightstand, or another spot that has meaning for you.

4. You can even place the knotted hair charm in a tree or other plant, such as a rose bush or heather shrub (depending on your objective). The plant's energy will contribute to your spell and help your intention materialize. Invite the nature fairies to assist you.

5. Leave a piece of jewelry for the merrow. If you've also sought aid from the nature spirits, leave them a gift of food and/or libation to thank them.

Numbers in Spellwork

Numbers are our most frequently used and familiar symbols. According to the study of numerology, each number has a unique resonance and meaning. Consequently, you can harness that energy in spellwork. Witches often use the number three to finalize a spell and bring it into manifestation—that's because we live in a three-dimensional world.

1: beginnings, action, individuality

2: partnership, duality, balance/imbalance

3: self-expression, manifestation, creativity

4: stability, permanence, solidity

5: change, movement, instability, communication

6: harmony, contentment, community, ideals

7: retreat, inner growth, spirituality

8: material gain, business success, financial security

9: completion, transition, wisdom, bridging the physical and spiritual realms

11: humanitarianism, spiritual growth, higher knowledge

22: spiritual power, work in the spirit world, managing occult forces

ROSE PETAL SPELL TO ATTRACT LOVE

Don't be misled by the simplicity of this spell—it can be just as effective as a long, complicated one. Your sincerity is what matters most. We associate roses with love and romance, so the symbolism will resonate with your subconscious. Invite the nature spirits, who care for flowers, to lend their energy to your spell.

You Will Need

- Pink rose petals
- Red rose petals
- A bowl or other container
- Food for the fairies

Directions

1. With your hands, combine the pink and red rose petals in the bowl. Red is the color of passion, pink the color of affection.

2. Sprinkle the petals outside your home. Or go to a place that has positive associations for you and sprinkle the petals there.

3. As you release them, say aloud:

    "I NOW ATTRACT A PARTNER WHO'S RIGHT FOR ME IN EVERY WAY
    AND FOR WHOM I'M RIGHT IN EVERY WAY."
    (If you prefer, compose your own affirmation or incantation.)

4. Don't specify a particular person you hope to attract. Not only is that manipulative, but you might limit yourself and prevent someone even better from coming along.

5. Leave food for the fairies to thank them for their assistance.

6. Repeat this procedure for three days in a row.

"This love is the rose that blooms forever."

JALAL AD-DIN MUHAMMAD RUMI, poet

FLORAL POTPOURRI TO ATTRACT LOVE

For witches on the go, here's another easy and effective floral spell to attract a romantic partner. Most likely, you know that roses are associated with love, but you may not be aware of some other flowers that can enhance loving feelings too. The Druids connected heather with luck in love. Jasmine inspires seduction and sensuality. Daisies foster friendship and fun in a romantic relationship. (See the Appendix for more flower characteristics.) Ask the nature fairies to join you.

You Will Need

- Dried rose petals in pink, red, orange, and other colors you like—each color has its own meanings
- Dried petals from any other flower you choose, such as myrtle, jasmine, daisies, or heather
- A pink or red bowl—if you can find one shaped like a heart, all the better
- 1 pink candle in a candleholder
- 1 red candle in a candleholder
- Matches or a lighter
- Food for the nature fairies

Directions

1. Put the dried flower petals in the bowl.

2. Set the candles on your altar or another surface where they can burn safely. Position them about 9 inches apart.

3. Set the bowl on your altar or other surface, between the candles.

4. Light the candles. As they burn, visualize a partner who is right for you in every way coming to you. Feel love and joy glowing and growing between you.

5. Spend as long as you like imagining this new love. The more vivid you can make your visualization, the stronger its power will be.

6. When you're ready, extinguish the candles.

7. Set the bowl on your nightstand or another spot in your bedroom.

8. Leave food for the fairies to thank them for their assistance.

TIE A LOVE NOTE ON A TREE

The Druids considered trees sacred, and associated particular qualities and powers with certain trees. The hawthorn, with its pink blossoms in the spring and red berries in autumn (sometimes called "pixie pears"), is said to have aphrodisiac properties. It's associated with Venus and Mars, the two planets that rule women and men, love and sex, respectively. In herbal medicine, it's used to treat heart conditions. This spell draws upon the hawthorn's magick to attract love into your life. The pixies and other nature spirits, who guard and nurture trees, can help.

You Will Need

- A piece of paper
- A pen, pencil, marker, or other writing utensil
- Rose, jasmine, or ylang-ylang essential oil
- A libation gift for the tree
- Food for the fairies

Directions

1. On the paper, write a love note to a prospective romantic partner, someone you don't know yet

2. Describe what you seek in a partner, as well as what you bring to the relationship. Be specific. I once asked for a romantic partner who liked to travel, but I forgot to add "with me." Soon I met a wonderful man who was a world traveler, but he preferred to travel alone.

3. Leave some things open for the universe to decide. Your ideal partner may have interests or qualities you haven't considered but that you may benefit from and enjoy. Maybe he's into Italian cuisine or she's a geology buff, and you can learn new things from each other.

4. When you've finished, dot each corner with essential oil and then fold the paper three times to secure the spell.

5. Place the love note in a hawthorn tree. (You may need to do some research to determine how to recognize a hawthorn tree

and where to find one.) As the paper deteriorates, it releases your message into the cosmos and sends your message to the person who's right for you.

6. Pour water, cider, wine, or another libation at the base of the tree to thank it for assisting you.

7. Set out food for the fairies as a thank-you gift.

> "Relationships are the Holy Spirit's laboratories in which He brings together people who have the maximal opportunity for mutual growth. He appraises who can learn most from whom at any given time, and then assigns them to each other."
>
> MARIANNE WILLIAMSON, *A Return to Love*

PLANT HEATHER FOR LUCK IN LOVE

Perhaps you've seen wild heather growing on the hills in Scotland. The Druids believed this pretty plant brought good luck in matters of the heart. It's hardy, fast-growing, and thrives in moist, acidic soil. If conditions are favorable in your locale, you can plant heather outdoors. Otherwise, you can grow it indoors—it doesn't get very tall, but it does need some sun. If you know feng shui, position the plant in the Relationship Gua of your home or yard. If you can't grow a live plant, download an image of one from the Internet. Ask the pixies and other nature spirits for their help.

You Will Need
- A heather seedling
- A trowel or shovel
- A container, if planting indoors
- Potting soil, if planting indoors
- A pen, pencil, marker, or crayon
- A picture of a heather plant from a book or downloaded from the Internet
- Food for the fairies

Directions

1. Plant the heather outdoors or in a container if you plan to grow it indoors.

2. Alternately, draw the Ogham letter *ura* beneath the picture of a heather shrub. Display the picture in your bedroom, the Relationship Gua of your home, or a place where you'll see it often.

3. Leave food outside to thank the fairies for their help.

CANDLE SPELL FOR A CLOSER RELATIONSHIP

The term candle comes from *candere,* a Latin word meaning "to shine" or "to make bright." Candles are the most common and versatile tools you're likely to use in your magick work, and they play a role in a lot of spells. They symbolize the fire element and Spirit, the energizing force that activates spells and rituals. Invite the fire spirits to participate in this spell to increase the closeness and happiness between you and a romantic partner. Sometimes called salamanders, these spirits can also add zing to a relationship that has grown a bit stale. Note: This spell takes six days to complete, so put the candles where you can leave them in place for that length of time.

You Will Need

- 1 candle to represent you—it should be of a color you like
- An athame, nail, nail file, ballpoint pen, or other sharp object
- 1 candle to represent your partner, in a color your partner likes
- Rose, ylang-ylang, musk, jasmine, or patchouli essential oil (or a blend)
- 2 candleholders
- Matches or a lighter
- A fire agate

Directions

1. On the candle that represents you, carve your initials with the sharp object.

2. Carve your partner's initials on the other candle.

3. Pour a little essential oil into your palm, and then dress the candles with it.

4. Fit the candles into their holders and set them on your altar or another place where they can burn safely. The candles should be at least 2 feet apart.

5. Light the candles. While they burn, envision love, affection, trust, comfort, romance, compassion, physical attraction—whatever you seek—glowing like a beautiful light between you and your partner.

6. Do this for at least 10 minutes, or as long as you like. Then extinguish the flames.

7. The next day, move the candles a little closer together.

8. Repeat steps 5 and 6.

9. Continue for four more days.

10. On the last (sixth) day of the spell, the candleholders should be touching. Allow the candles to finish burning down completely. Caution: Never leave burning candles unattended.

11. Leave the fire agate for the fairies as a thank-you gift.

CREATE A FAIRY BOX

This practice is intended to enhance an existing romantic relationship or to attract new love, but you can adapt it for use in any area of your life. By creating an ongoing source of gifts for the fae, you invite them to continue helping you in your partnership(s). The merrows might agree to assist you in this endeavor—they're fond of jewels and other treasure, plus they know the secrets of love, sex, and seduction.

You Will Need

- Pictures that represent love to you (from magazines, greeting cards, or downloaded from the Internet)

- Rubber cement, a glue stick, or other adhesive
- A heart-shaped or circular cardboard box with a lid (you can purchase these in stores that sell craft supplies)
- Rose, jasmine, ylang-ylang, musk, or patchouli essential oil
- Slips of paper
- A pen, pencil, marker, or other writing utensil
- Small, glitzy objects for the fairies

Directions

1. Sort through the images you've collected; decide which ones you plan to use and how you want to arrange them on your fairy box.

2. Affix the pictures to the box in a way you find appealing. If you like, you can add words, poems, affirmations, etc.

3. When you're happy with your fairy box, put three dots of essential oil on it. If the box is a heart, put a dab in each of the curved sections at the top and in the pointed part.

4. On a slip of paper, write something you'd like to experience in a romantic relationship, either a new love you hope to attract or an existing partnership. Keep it short and to the point, for example: "Go dancing regularly" or "Share chores more equitably" or "Take an enjoyable trip together."

5. On a Friday (the day astrologers say is ruled by Venus, planet of love and relationships), put one slip of paper with one request written on it in the fairy box.

6. Add a gift for the fairies, such as a shiny coin, a small crystal, or a piece of costume jewelry (this is a good way to repurpose those single earrings that have lost their mates).

7. Speak to the fairies and explain that they can take one of the gifts in the box in return for fulfilling one of your wishes.

8. Repeat each day for a week. Add a different written intention and another gift for the fae each day.

9. At the end of the week, open the box and see if any/how many of the gifts have been claimed by the fairies. How many of your wishes have been fulfilled? Don't worry if it seems like nothing

has happened yet; it may take a while for the fairies to catch on—especially if you've just begun working with them. Before long, you'll notice results.

10. If by chance the gifts in your fairy box are mounting up and it doesn't seem like the fae are participating, take the objects from the box and place them in various locations outdoors. Then start again on the next Friday.

Doing Spells with a Partner

When it comes to doing magick, two hearts can be better than one—provided both parties are in agreement. The blend of yin and yang energies forms a strong, balanced creative force. Doing a spell with a partner to increase the love between you can be a very powerful and beautiful experience. Many couples do magick together to conceive a child, to attract prosperity, or for other joint purposes. Before you begin, discuss your intentions and your feelings about the spell you plan to do. Each of you should have input in designing and casting the spell. Remember, the outcome will affect both of you.

ROSE MASSAGE OIL

This massage oil gets its power from two ingredients we associate with love: roses and rose quartz. Invite a merrow to join you in formulating the magick oil.

You Will Need
- A glass bottle or jar with a lid
- 3 ounces of your favorite massage oil, or use olive, coconut, or jojoba oil
- A few drops of rose essential oil (whatever amount smells right to you)
- 2 small pieces of tumbled rose quartz
- A piece of pink paper (about 2 inches by 2 inches) to use as a label
- A pen or marker that writes red ink
- Tape

Directions

1. Wash the bottle or jar with mild soap and water.

2. Pour the massage or vegetable oil into the bottle or jar.

3. Add the rose essential oil.

4. Add one piece of rose quartz.

5. On the piece of pink paper draw the symbol for the planet Venus, which astrologers say governs love and relationships.

6. Tape the label to the bottle, with the image facing in. It will imprint the oil with your intention.

7. Put the lid on the bottle or jar and shake it three times to charge the mixture.

8. Leave the second piece of rose quartz for the merrow to thank her for her assistance.

9. Enjoy a romantic massage with your partner.

USE A TAROT CARD TO SWEETEN A RELATIONSHIP

Many witches use the beautiful oracle known as the tarot for readings, meditation, and spellwork. The powerful imagery on the cards speaks directly to your subconscious and strengthens your focus. Ask an undine to participate in creating this sweet love potion. Prepare it during the full moon.

You Will Need
- The Two of Cups from a tarot deck
- A bottle of sweet wine (red, white, or rosé, whichever you prefer) or a bottle of sparkling apple cider
- A chalice or glass/crystal goblet

Directions

1. On the night of a full moon, lay the tarot card faceup on a windowsill, preferably where the moon can shine on it.

2. Set the unopened bottle of wine or cider on the card. The romantic imagery on the card will imprint the sweet beverage with your intention to sweeten a relationship.

3. Allow the bottle and card to remain like this overnight.

4. In the morning, return the card to your tarot deck.

5. The next night, open the wine or cider and pour some of it into your chalice or goblet.

6. Ideally, you'll want to share the drink with your partner. If that's not possible, you can drink it yourself.

7. Enjoy the magick libation for three consecutive nights.

8. Save some of the beverage and pour it in a body of water as an offering for the undines to thank them.

The Origins of the Tarot

For hundreds of years, people have turned to the tarot for advice, guidance, and answers to important questions. Many theories exist about the oracle's beginnings. One says the cards date back more than two thousand years to ancient Egypt and the great library in Alexandria. Another story tells us the Crusaders brought the tarot back with them from the Middle East. Yet another credits the Romani people with introducing the cards into Europe.

In her book *The Sacred Circle Tarot*, Anna Franklin writes that Celtic scholar and author "R.J. Stewart suggests that the tarot had its origins in 'the storytelling traditions and images preserved by travelling entertainers, originally the bards or *filid* of Celtic culture.' He points out that the images of the tarot have clear connections with images described in the *Vita Merlini*, a text that pre-dates the earliest known tarot deck by three centuries."

TAROT SPELL FOR A FINANCIALLY LUCRATIVE PARTNERSHIP

Here's another spell that taps the magickal imagery and meaning of the tarot. This one uses the Ten of Pentacles to attract a new partnership that benefits you financially, or to improve the financial situation in an existing relationship. In some tarot decks, including the Rider-Waite-Smith deck and the Gilded Tarot, this card shows a happy couple standing amid lush vegetation as they observe their luxurious home. A merrow can help you with this spell.

You Will Need

- The Ten of Pentacles from a tarot deck
- Rose, ylang-ylang, jasmine, or musk essential oil
- 1 gold-colored candle
- 1 silver-colored candle
- 2 candleholders
- A piece of jewelry, the glitzier the better
- Matches or a lighter

Directions

1. Remove the Ten of Pentacles card from a tarot deck. Set it faceup on your altar, a table, or another flat surface. This spell takes three days to complete, so you'll need to work in a spot where you can leave everything in place for that amount of time.

2. Pour a little essential oil into your palm and dress the candles with it.

3. Fit the candles into their holders and set them on your altar, table, or other surface. Set the gold candle to the right of the tarot card, and the silver candle to the left of the card.

4. Place the piece of jewelry above the tarot card.

5. Light the candles and let them burn for at least 10 minutes, while you envision yourself enjoying a mutually joyful, fulfilling relationship rich with abundance of all kinds. When you've finished, snuff out the candles.

6. Repeat this the next day/night and the day/night after that.

7. At the end of the three days, leave the piece of jewelry outdoors on a rock or tree stump for the merrow. Or, toss it in a body of water—she's a water fairy, after all, so she'll find it.

CREATE A LOVE TALISMAN

What's the difference between an amulet and a talisman? An amulet repels or protects against something; a talisman attracts something. This talisman brings good fortune and happiness in a romantic partnership. Ask a merrow or korrigan to assist you with making it.

You Will Need

- Dried petals from two or more of these flowers: rose, daisy, pink clover, jasmine, heather, myrtle, or geranium
- A rose-colored drawstring pouch, preferably one made of silk
- A small vial of rose, jasmine, or ylang-ylang essential oil
- 1 piece of rose quartz
- 1 piece of carnelian
- A silver heart-shaped charm
- A piece of pink paper
- A pen or marker that writes red ink
- Matches or a lighter
- Sandalwood incense in a holder

Directions

1. Put the dried flower petals in the pouch.

2. Rub a little essential oil on the rose quartz and the carnelian, and add them to the pouch. Rose quartz brings love and affection; carnelian brings passion and enthusiasm.

3. Dot the charm with a little oil and add it to the pouch.

4. On the piece of paper, write the top three qualities you seek in a mate. Then draw three Xs on the paper. We think of X as a symbol for a kiss, but it's also the Norse rune for partnership.

5. Fold the paper three times and slip it into the pouch.

6. Tie three knots to close the pouch. As you tie each knot, say aloud:

> "I NOW ENJOY A LOVE THAT'S RIGHT FOR ME IN EVERY WAY."
> (Or, compose your own affirmation.)

7. Light the incense and hold the talisman in the smoke to charge it.

8. Empty the remaining essential oil in a body of water as a gift for the fairies who helped you.

9. Carry the talisman with you to bring happiness and good fortune in a relationship.

RIBBON SPELL TO ATTRACT FRIENDS

For many of us, friends are just as important as lovers or family. As Jess C. Scott said, "Friends are the family you choose." This spell is a good one to do when you move to a new place, start attending a new school, or begin a new job, but you can do it whenever you want to meet people with whom you feel a special kinship. Ask the air fairies known as sylphs to carry your request for friendship to the people who will be right for you.

You Will Need

- 12-inch-long ribbons, as many as you like—choose at least one of each color of the rainbow
- A marker that will write on fabric
- Tape
- A shoebox or other container

Directions

1. On each ribbon, write a quality you seek in a friend. It might be loyalty, patience, compassion, understanding, cheerfulness, honesty—whatever you value in other people.

2. On one yellow ribbon, write "Thank you."

3. Go to the sector of your home that feng shui practitioners associate with friendship. When you stand at the door you use most often to enter your home and look in, this sector is at the far right of your house or apartment.

4. Tape the ribbons to a window in this sector, with the words you've written on them facing out.

5. Take the yellow ribbon on which you wrote "Thank you" outside and tie it on a tree. This is your gift to the sylphs for their help.

6. When you've established friendships you enjoy, remove the ribbons from your window. Write your friends' names on the ribbons that best express their qualities. Store the ribbons in a shoebox or other container.

SPELL TO END A RELATIONSHIP PEACEFULLY

Sometimes it becomes necessary to end a relationship. Even though the separation may be painful, it needn't be acrimonious. This spell lets you bring a peaceful close to the partnership, so you can heal and move on. You can ask the fairies for help in making this break, but they won't understand your feelings—they don't experience emotions the way we do. However, their detachment may show you how to let go of old ties instead of allowing them to limit you.

You Will Need
- A piece of rope or cord, 2 feet long
- Scissors or a knife (if your athame is sharp enough, you can use it)
- A cauldron, barbecue grill, hibachi, or fireplace
- Firewood—a combination of pine, oak, and apple is ideal
- Matches or a lighter
- A photo of you and your partner
- Lavender flowers
- Basil (optional)

Directions

1. Tie a knot in the rope or cord. This symbolizes the bond between you and your partner.

2. Close your eyes and imagine you are holding one end of the rope and your partner is holding the other end. Feel the tension, restriction, or other uncomfortable sensation associated with the relationship.

3. When you feel ready, open your eyes and cut the rope in two. You may experience a sense of sadness, remorse, or even a slight pain as you do this.

4. In the spot you've chosen where you can burn a fire safely, lay the wood you've gathered. Pine represents purification and cleansing; oak symbolizes strength; apple has associations with love and peace.

5. When the fire is established, put the photo of you and your soon-to-be-former partner in the flames. As it burns, envision the relationship ending, turning to ash.

6. Next, lay the rope that formerly tied you together in the fire. As it burns, feel the freedom and release that come from ending this relationship that no longer serves you.

7. When the rope has finished burning, toss the lavender flowers into the flames. Lavender has calming, healing, soothing properties that can ease the distress of a breakup and smooth the way for future growth. It also encourages peace and forgiveness. As it burns, you may feel animosity, regrets, resentment, or other unpleasant feelings dissipating.

8. If you sense any potential threat or harm connected with the end of this relationship, sprinkle basil in the flames to provide protection. (You may also want to do one or more of the other protection spells in this book or in other books in the Modern Witchcraft series.) If necessary, contact authorities who can provide protection.

9. Allow the fire to burn down completely. When the ashes have cooled, collect them and take them to a place away from your

home. Scatter them on the ground in a barren spot, away from water or trees. This symbolizes laying to rest the remains of the relationship.

10. As you do this final step in the spell, consider offering a blessing to this person with whom you once knew happiness. Thank him or her for the good times you shared, the lessons you learned, the growth that came through the partnership. Wish the person well and ask that peace be between you, now and always.

Chapter 7

WORKING WITH FAIRIES FOR PROSPERITY AND ABUNDANCE

W hile we live on Planet Earth in physical form, we require money and material possessions to survive. How much and what kinds will vary from person to person, and will likely change at different stages in our lives. Money isn't everything, of course, and we know it can't bring love, health, friendship, or peace of mind, but having enough to meet your needs makes life easier. When you're constantly worried about paying bills or when you spend the bulk of your time just eking out a living, you don't have the energy or space to pursue other interests.

Abundance and prosperity are more than money, however. When you perform prosperity magick, the energy you raise and manipulate can attract wealth in forms other than money that will make your life more comfortable. As a witch, you also realize that your attitude influences your ability to receive the abundance you seek. That's the Law of Attraction—whatever you focus your attention on, you attract. Many of us have been taught erroneous ideas about money, such as money is the root of all evil, and those self-limiting conceptions block prosperity.

When you perform the spells and rituals in this chapter, take a tip from the fairies. They don't hold negative ideas about their self-worth, they don't feel guilty about receiving bounty, nor do they compare their wealth to anyone else's. Here's another thought to remember: The universe is infinite and will give you what you believe you deserve, without disadvantaging anyone else.

> "When you think a sustained thought it is immediately sent out into the Universe. That thought magnetically attaches itself to the *like* frequency, and then within seconds sends the reading of that frequency back to you through your feelings."
>
> JACK CANFIELD, *The Secret*

FINDING WEALTH

Which fairies can help you attract wealth and other forms of abundance? Which can boost your prosperity consciousness and your sense of financial well-being?

- **LEPRECHAUNS:** Leprechauns know where the gold is buried, and if you treat them right they can help you acquire your share of treasure. Legends say leprechauns won't lie, but they may not be straightforward with you—be sure to word your requests carefully and pay close attention to a leprechaun's "promises."

- **ELVES:** Known for their craftsmanship and work ethic, elves can help you prosper in your career. Petition their assistance if you seek a better job, a raise, or a promotion. Don't ask them to get involved in a get-rich-quick scheme or anything underhanded, though. They can also show you how to use your skills to your best advantage and to develop talents you may not have realized you possessed.

- **PIXIES:** Green witches, especially, can benefit from working with these nature fairies. Invite them to assist you with botanical spells for prosperity. Pixies are fond of essential oils—the fragrances will attract them to spells that involve scent.

- **MERROWS:** Legends say these water fairies possess great wealth, having salvaged the treasure from sunken ships. Tales of human men marrying merrows and enriching themselves in the process abound in folklore. But you don't need to marry a merrow to gain her money. You can work with her in a cooperative venture or other type of partnership, to mutual advantage.

POTION TO ENHANCE A PROSPERITY CONSCIOUSNESS

Before you can attract prosperity, you have to believe you deserve it. Are negative ideas about money hampering your ability to receive the abundance you desire? This magick potion helps dispel self-limiting ideas and boosts your sense of self-worth. Ask a merrow to join you in preparing the potion. Note: The spell takes seven days to complete.

You Will Need

- 1 agate (green)
- 1 aventurine
- 1 garnet
- 1 jade
- 1 peridot
- 1 tiger's eye
- 1 turquoise
- A green glass bottle or jar with a lid
- 8 ounces of spring water
- 2 gold-colored candles in candleholders
- Peppermint essential oil
- Matches or a lighter
- A chalice or glass

Directions

1. Collect the seven gemstones and wash them with mild soap and water. The stones should be small enough to fit easily into the bottle or jar. Choose stones that don't have holes in them—drilling holes through gems can destroy their power.

2. Wash the bottle or jar and pour the water into it.

3. On the first day, drop one of the gemstones into the bottle or jar, then cap it.

4. Set the candles about 8 inches apart on your altar, a table, or other surface where they can burn safely.

5. Dress the candles with a little bit of the oil (don't put oil on the wicks) and then light them.

6. Set the bottle or jar between the candles.

7. Let the candles burn for at least 10 minutes. Inhale the fresh, clean, stimulating scent of peppermint.

8. Call up one old, outdated, self-limiting thought that may be inhibiting your ability to attract abundance. Envision the peppermint scent clearing away that idea. Imagine the golden glow of the

candles replacing it with self-confidence, optimism, or another positive attitude.

9. When you feel ready or your attention begins to wander, snuff out the candles.

10. On the second day, repeat this ritual. Add another one of the gemstones to the bottle or jar. Clear away another tired old thought and replace it with a new, bright one.

11. Repeat the ritual each day, until you've added all the stones to the bottle or jar.

12. On the seventh day, strain out the stones and pour the water into your chalice or glass. Drink the energized water, imprinted with the power of the gemstones, and feel it strengthening your prosperity consciousness.

13. Give one or more of the gemstones to the merrow to thank her for helping you.

14. Save the other gemstones to use in future spells.

PLANT HERBS FOR PROSPERITY

You're probably familiar with tales of leprechauns and their pots of gold. These legendary Irish fairies can, indeed, bring you money and abundance of all kinds—if it suits them—but they're notorious tricksters who don't share their wealth willingly. Folklore says that in order to win a leprechaun's gold, you first have to catch him—he'll pay his captor handsomely to let him go. This spell, however, doesn't try to part the fairy from his treasure. Instead, it appeals to his role as a nature spirit and guardian of the earth's bounty.

You Will Need

- A garden plot or a ceramic flowerpot
- Potting soil, if you're using a flowerpot
- A garden trowel or shovel
- A silver dollar or other coin
- Mint, parsley, or dill seeds
- Water
- A glass of ale and/or some natural tobacco

Directions

1. Envision yourself surrounded by pure white light and say aloud this protection affirmation (or another you've composed yourself):

> "I AM PROTECTED BY DIVINE WHITE LIGHT.
> I AM SAFE AND SOUND AT ALL TIMES AND IN ALL SITUATIONS."

2. Invite a leprechaun to assist you in fulfilling this spell. Sense his presence nearby. You may see a flash of green, hear him laugh, or smell smoke from his briar pipe.

3. Speak to him with respect and assure him that you mean him no harm. Acknowledge his ability to make plants grow strong and healthy. Ask him to nurture these seeds and to bring you the wealth you seek, without engaging in any mischief.

4. If you are working in a garden plot, dig a hole deep enough to plant the seeds you've chosen to grow.

5. Place the coin in the bottom of the hole to signify your intention.

6. If you are using a flowerpot, lay the coin in the bottom, then fill the pot with soil.

7. Plant the herb seeds, according to instructions on the package.

8. Water the seeds while you visualize them growing and thriving. Say aloud:

> "As THIS PLANT GROWS, SO DOES MY PROSPERITY.
> THIS IS DONE IN HARMONY WITH DIVINE WILL,
> MY OWN TRUE WILL, AND WITH GOOD TO ALL."
> (Or, compose your own affirmation.)

9. Place the ale and/or tobacco on the ground or beside the flowerpot as a gift for the leprechaun to thank him for his assistance. Soon, you'll notice it has disappeared.

10. Continue watering and caring for your plant(s). Each time you clip its leaves to eat, thank the plant and envision abundance flowing to you from all directions.

HANG TREE OFFERINGS FOR FAIRIES

The ancient Celts considered trees sacred. Each tree had a special significance and distinctive characteristics, as well as magickal powers. The mighty oak, or *duir*, is associated with the Druids. Often Celtic ceremonies and rites were held in groves of trees. In the Irish alphabet known as Ogham, each letter corresponds to a tree (see Chapter 4).

Ask the fairies, especially the pixies, to assist you in attracting abundance of all kinds. By presenting them and the wildlife they protect with gifts of food, you'll gain the favor of nature fairies and encourage them to reciprocate. Your offerings will be especially welcome during the cold winter months, when food is scarce.

You Will Need

- Fruit, nuts, bread—whatever foods the wildlife in your area like to eat (you may want to make strings of popcorn or cranberries to hang in trees)
- String to hang food on the trees
- Food for the fairies

Directions

1. Hang your offerings on a tree(s). Use biodegradable string or other materials to fasten the food to the branches. If you prefer, you can purchase or make feeders for the birds.

2. Leave food for the fairies too. They're especially fond of honey cake and other sweets. (German fairies enjoy strudel; Greek fairies love baklava.)

3. In return for your gifts, ask the fairies to bring you good fortune in the coming year.

Holly Bushes

Legends say that fairies take shelter under holly bushes during the cold winter months. If you have a holly in your yard, or know of a place where a holly grows, put food under its spiky leaves as a gift for the fairies.

SPELL TO FIND A LOST ITEM

Do you seem to keep losing things? It may not be your memory that's failing. Instead of wasting money replacing things you can't find, talk to the fairies. Nothing is ever really lost, although things do go missing. Pixies like to play tricks on humans, and they're known to "borrow" stuff. They're not usually being malicious, though, and you may be able to negotiate a swap to get them to return the item. Instead of searching diligently for your keys, glasses, or another "misplaced" object, try asking the pixies for help.

You Will Need

- Gifts for the pixies—they like milk and honey, cake, and cookies

Directions

1. Close your eyes, take a few slow, deep breaths, and let your mind relax.

2. Explain to the pixies that you'd really like to have the missing object back and that you'll give them something in exchange. Be quiet and listen—they may tell you what they'd like as a gift.

3. Ask them to show you where the object you seek is. Be patient and allow an image of the item to emerge in your awareness.

4. When you see or sense a place, open your eyes and go look there— even if you've checked that spot before.

5. If the object is truly yours, it will come back to you. (If it doesn't, accept that someone else needed it more, or that it's time to release what once belonged to you.)

6. When you find the item, give the fairies a gift in return for their assistance.

DESIGN A SIGIL TO ATTRACT WEALTH

A sigil is a symbol you draw in order to produce a specific result. In a sense, a sigil is a way of communicating with yourself via secret code, because no one else can interpret the symbol. Although there are various techniques for designing sigils, the easiest one involves fashioning an image from letters. Consider asking the elemental fairies of the air and earth to assist you—air fairies are adept at communication; earth fairies understand how to manifest intentions in the physical world.

You Will Need

- A piece of paper
- A pen, pencil, marker, or crayon—choose a color you like or one that represents wealth to you, such as gold or silver
- Food for the fairies

Directions

1. Start by writing a word or a short affirmation that states your intention, for example, "wealth" or "prosperity."

2. Next, draw an image using the letters. Entwine the letters to form a symbol. You can use upper- and/or lowercase letters, block or script. Position them right-side up, upside down, forward, or backward.

3. The end result depicts your objective in a graphic manner that your subconscious understands, although it won't make sense to anyone else.

4. Display the sigil in a place where you will see it often—on your altar, by your computer, etc. You might even want to photograph the sigil with your phone so you can look at it regularly. Each time you look at the sigil, you'll instantly recognize its meaning at a deep level, and that will reinforce your intention.

5. Leave food for the fairies to thank them for helping you.

WRITE LEAF LETTERS TO FAIRIES

Pixies, who care for the plant world, will understand this form of communication better than a text or email. Ask the fairies to help you increase your prosperity, but don't specify exactly how you expect that to happen. For example, don't say you want to earn more money, because that limits the possibility of receiving money in other ways.

You Will Need

- 8 leaves from a tree or other plant
- 4 ounces of red wine or another libation, such as apple cider
- A marker that will write on any material
- Cake, cookies, or other sweets

Directions

1. Ask a tree (or other plant) for permission to take eight of its leaves. Eight is the number of financial gain and stability. If you sense the tree agreeing, snip off the leaves. If not, ask another tree (or plant) until you find one that is willing to assist you.

2. Thank the tree and pour the wine or other libation near the base of the tree.

3. On each leaf, write a word or brief affirmation stating your intention, for example, wealth, prosperity, abundance, etc. You may write the same thing on all eight leaves or something different on each one.

4. When you've finished, take the leaves and the sweets outside to your yard, a park, or another place in nature.

5. Call to the pixies, out loud or mentally. Request their assistance and assure them that the money or other form of abundance should come to you in harmony with Divine Will, harming none.

6. When you sense the pixies nearby, agreeing to assist you, scatter the leaves on the ground.

7. Crumble the cake, cookies, or other sweets and scatter them among the leaves as a thank-you gift for the fairies.

USE ABUNDANCE CRYSTALS TO ATTRACT WEALTH

Abundance crystals have inclusions of a green mineral called chlorite. Some of them even have smaller crystals growing inside of them. These quartz crystals are uniquely suited to attract abundance of all kinds, hence their name. Ask a pixie, merrow, or leprechaun to participate in your spellcasting. When you're working with the fae, however, you'll need to keep a close eye on your abundance crystals—fairies love them and will make off with them if they get a chance. They've absconded with several of mine—fortunately only the smaller ones.

You Will Need

- 3 abundance crystals
- Peppermint essential oil
- 2 green candles in candleholders
- A silver dollar or other coin—rare, unique, or valuable coins are preferable to pennies or dimes, simply because they have more appeal for you, and thereby strengthen your intention
- Matches or a lighter
- A crystal for the fairy who helps you
- 4 iron nails or other pieces of iron
- A piece of black silk

Directions

1. Perform this spell between the new moon and the full moon, when the moon is waxing.

2. Set the three abundance crystals on your altar, table, or other flat surface. Arrange them in a triangular pattern so that each crystal is about 3 inches away from the others. (Three is a number of manifestation in the three-dimensional world.)

3. Dot each crystal with the oil.

4. Set one candle at the left of the crystal triangle and one to the right.

5. Place the coin in the center of the crystal triangle.

6. Light the candles. As they burn, see the crystals sparkle in the candlelight. You may notice fairies dancing in the crystals and/or in the candle flames.

7. Envision the crystals sending out vibes that connect with all sorts of abundance from all corners of the earth. Visualize that abundance flowing toward you.

8. Say an affirmation aloud, such as:

"I NOW RECEIVE ABUNDANCE OF ALL KINDS AT ALL TIMES, ALWAYS AND ALWAYS. THIS IS IN HARMONY WITH DIVINE WILL, MY OWN TRUE WILL, AND WITH GOOD TO ALL, HARMING NONE. SO MOTE IT BE."
(Or, compose your own affirmation or incantation.)

9. When you start to lose your focus, extinguish the candles. Pick up the three crystals and the coin.

10. Leave the crystal you've chosen for the fairy on your altar as a thank-you gift.

11. Wrap the coin and one of the iron nails in the piece of black silk to protect the coin from fairy thieves (unless it's not a particularly valuable coin, in which case you may choose to leave it for them as a gift). If the coin is rare or valuable, consider storing it in a safe deposit box at your bank.

12. Set the three abundance crystals in places that can help to generate wealth for you. You might want to put one on your desk, beside your computer, on your altar, or in what feng shui calls the Wealth Gua. (When you stand at the entrance to your home or workplace looking in, the sector that relates to wealth is at the far left-hand corner.)

13. Place an iron nail beside each crystal to keep the fairies from appropriating it.

What's in Your Crystal?

Pick up a crystal and examine it closely. Look first at its surface: the planes that form its sides and points. Then, gaze more deeply into its interior. Within the crystal's body you may notice tiny silvery sheets or flakes, wispy streaks that look like smoke, perhaps clouds, snow, birds, angels, or rainbows. Some crystals contain bits of plant or mineral material, or smaller crystals growing inside them. You might even see whole landscapes or galaxies in your crystal.

These details give a crystal certain attributes and potentials. They tell you what the crystal can do, how it expresses itself, and how it can work with you. Each feature indicates an area of specialty. Many crystals embody several of the features mentioned above, which makes them adept at handling a variety of tasks.

USE THE TAROT TO BRING GOOD FORTUNE

Many witches use the tarot to gain advice, for meditation, and to peek into the future. You can also use this beautiful oracle in spellwork. The vibrant imagery on the cards stimulates your intuition and sends visual directions to your subconscious. This spell draws upon a practice engaged in by the Spanish nobility as a form of entertainment during the fifteenth century. These Renaissance tarot fanciers wrote verses on the cards—each verse contained the same number of lines as the number of the card. Because we connect leprechauns with good luck, they're the most logical choice among the members of the fairy world to help with this spell.

You Will Need
- The Nine of Cups tarot card
- A pen or permanent marker
- A bell
- Natural tobacco and/or a glass of ale

Directions
1. From a tarot deck you don't use for readings, select the Nine of Cups, often referred to as the "wish card." Many witches keep one or more tarot decks to use specifically in spellcraft, in addition to the decks with which they do readings. If you prefer, you can download an image of this card from the Internet.

2. Gaze at the card for a few moments. This is considered one of the most auspicious cards in the tarot. Let its positive imagery send a message to your subconscious that whatever you wish for will be yours.

3. Think about nine things you want in connection with prosperity and abundance. These can be material goodies you desire, such

as a new car. Maybe you seek fortunate opportunities that will advance your career. Enjoying a comfortable and fulfilling lifestyle may be important to you. Perhaps "abundance" has a broader meaning to you that includes good health, friends, etc.

4. When you've decided on nine wishes, write the first one on the face of the tarot card. This should be the most important of your wishes, what matters most to you. Either write a word or two, or pen a phrase that describes your intention as an affirmation (see the sidebar later in this chapter: What's the Difference Between an Affirmation and an Incantation?). For example, you might write "I now acquire a new Mercedes-Benz GLE" or "I now pay off the mortgage on my house."

5. After you write your wish, ring the bell. This alerts your mind to act on what you've just written, while also grounding your thoughts in the here and now. Sound adds another sensory component to your spell too. It also marks the steps in this spell, in much the same way as ringing bells cue participants in a spiritual ritual to move to the next step.

6. Write your second-most important wish on the card, beneath the first. Again, this might be a word or two, or a phrase in the form of an affirmation that describes your intention.

7. After you've written your wish, ring the bell.

8. Repeat these steps until you've written all nine wishes on the tarot card.

9. Set out the tobacco and/or ale to thank the leprechaun for his assistance. You may smell the smoke of his briar pipe, hear his laughter, or even see a four-leaf clover indicating he's processing your "orders" and all is well.

10. Display the card where you'll see it often. If you like, carry it in your wallet or purse.

COMBINE CRYSTALS AND TAROT CARDS TO GENERATE PROSPERITY

Crystals are among the most prized tools in a witch's collection, in part because they're so versatile. They can attract, direct, store, and amplify energy. They can aid healing on every level. They can enhance the powers of other crystals and gemstones. They can serve as portals into the fairy realm and other worlds. And much more. This spell brings together the tarot and crystals to generate prosperity. However, you can easily adapt this spell for other purposes by simply substituting a different tarot card. The crystal will absorb the symbolism of the card and transmit it. Earth fairies, including leprechauns and pixies, can assist you in this spell.

You Will Need

- 1 clear quartz crystal
- The Nine of Pentacles tarot card
- A piece of black fabric, preferably silk
- A crystal for the fairy who aids you

Directions

1. Choose a clear quartz crystal you sense will happily work in conjunction with you to help you prosper. A creator/manifester crystal is your best bet. It has either another smaller crystal growing inside it, like a pregnant woman, or a number of smaller crystals grouped around its base, like a mother with many children.

2. Choose a Nine of Pentacles card from a tarot deck that feels right to you for this spell—it needn't be one you use for readings or even your favorite deck. What matters is that the imagery on the card appeals to you. This card represents fulfillment, accomplishing your goals, and reaping the rewards you deserve.

3. Cleanse the crystal with mild soap and water to remove any vibrations that might interfere with your spellwork.

4. Hold the crystal to your third eye and envision what you desire. Then hold the crystal to your lips and tell it what you want it to do.

5. Lay the tarot card faceup on your altar or another surface.

6. Set the crystal on the card.

7. Cover the card and crystal with the piece of black fabric and leave it overnight.

8. In the morning, remove the fabric and return the tarot card to its deck.

9. Leave the crystal you've chosen as a gift for the fairy on a rock, tree stump, earthen mound, or other place where they're sure to find it.

10. Carry the creator/manifester crystal, imprinted with your intention, in your pocket or purse to bring you prosperity.

MAKE A GEMSTONE TALISMAN TO ATTRACT PROSPERITY

Gemstones have long been treasured for their beauty but also as a commodity. Therefore, witches often include them in prosperity spells. Each gem has its own special meaning. For this talisman you'll collect several different stones, combining their magickal properties to suit your needs. Invite a leprechaun or a merrow to join you in crafting this spell.

- **AGATE (GREEN):** Helps stabilize your finances
- **AVENTURINE:** Attracts wealth and abundance
- **GARNET:** Inspires creativity and boosts manifestation
- **JADE:** Brings good luck and success in financial areas
- **LABRADORITE:** Protects against financial losses
- **OBSIDIAN (BLACK):** Instills practicality and stability in money matters
- **PERIDOT:** Attracts wealth and confers high status to the wearer
- **TIGER'S EYE:** Increases good fortune and prosperity
- **TURQUOISE:** Brings luck and protection

Magickal Turquoise

According to Robert Simmons and Naisha Ahsian, coauthors of *The Book of Stones*, turquoise has been used longer than any other stone for jewelry, talismans and amulets, healing, and trade. Turquoise beads at least seven thousand years old have been found in Iraq. The Egyptians mined the stone in 3200 B.C.E., and the indigenous people of the American Southwest were working with it more than three thousand years ago.

You Will Need

- 3 or more of the stones from the previous list
- A green, gold, or silver drawstring pouch
- A stone for the fairy who assists you

Directions

1. Put the gemstones you've selected in the pouch.

2. Tie the pouch shut with eight knots. Eight is the number of material prosperity.

3. Carry this talisman in your pocket or purse to attract wealth. If you prefer, put it in your desk drawer. If you work in a retail business, place it in your cash register.

4. To thank each of the fairies who've assisted you, offer each of them one stone.

CAULDRON SPELL TO SPEED PROSPERITY

Do you need cash in a hurry? Is your financial situation sluggish? This spell uses fire as well as spicy-hot ingredients to heat up your prospects and speed things along. Invite the earth and fire spirits to join you in casting this spell.

You Will Need

- A cauldron (you can use a hibachi, fireplace, or fire pit if you don't have a cauldron)
- Cedar wood
- Matches or a lighter
- Powdered ginger
- Cinnamon
- Cayenne pepper
- Dry mustard
- Cloves
- Food for the fairies

Directions

1. In the cauldron, lay the cedar wood and light a fire.

2. When the fire is well established, toss the spices into the flames, one at a time. You should add at least 1 teaspoon of each spice.

3. Allow the fire to burn completely. (Caution: Don't leave a burning fire unattended.)

4. Let the ashes cool, then scatter them at the base of a cedar tree.

5. Leave food outside on a rock or tree stump to thank the fairies.

SPELL TO SECURE YOUR MONEY

Does it seem that no matter what you earn, money keeps going out faster than it comes in? Do you have trouble saving for unexpected expenses? Is it hard for you to resist the urge to buy things you don't really need? If so, this spell can help you hold on to your money and start saving instead of only spending. Request assistance from a leprechaun: Their savvy in money matters is legendary.

You Will Need

- A likeness of a million-dollar bill—you can download this from the Internet
- A black marker
- Pine essential oil
- A black ribbon 4 inches long
- A small metal box
- 1 piece of green agate
- A shovel or trowel
- 1 large stone
- Natural tobacco (without synthetic chemicals or pesticides)

Directions

1. On the bill, write your full name.

2. Dot each corner of the bill with the essential oil.

3. Roll the bill tightly.

4. Tie the rolled bill with the black ribbon. As you knot the ribbon, say aloud:

"MY MONEY IS SAFE AND SECURE. I HAVE MORE THAN ENOUGH FOR
EVERYTHING I NEED AND WANT, AND PLENTY TO SHARE WITH OTHERS.
SO MOTE IT BE."
(Or, compose your own affirmation.)

5. Place the rolled bill in the metal box.

6. Put the agate in the box to stabilize your finances.

7. Bury the box in your yard, or take it to a place that has meaning
   for you and bury it near a tree.

8. Place a large stone on top of the spot where you've hidden your
   "money."

9. Ask the leprechaun to protect it for you. Sprinkle the tobacco on
   the ground as a thank-you gift for the fairy.

PROSPERITY TEA

This tasty tea has healthy properties as well as magickal ones—you can
drink it to soothe digestive complaints as well as to attract wealth. Enjoy
it hot in cool months or iced in the summer. The nature spirits, who guide
and nurture all of earth's plants, can boost the benefits of this potion.

You Will Need
- Hot water
- Dried peppermint leaves
- Ginger, fresh minced is best, but you can use dried ginger
  instead or purchase tea bags that combine both spices
- A sieve
- A cup or glass with no images or words on it
- Lemon juice
- Honey
- A spoon, preferably silver or silverplate
- Food for the fairies

Directions
1. To hot water, add dried peppermint leaves and ginger. Witches
   associate mint with prosperity, and spicy ginger speeds up the

action of any potion. Let the herbs steep for a few minutes until they infuse the water with their flavors and healing properties.

2. Strain out the plant material (if you've used tea bags, discard them).

3. Pour the herb-infused water into a cup. Add lemon juice and honey to taste.

4. With the spoon, stir the lemon juice and honey in a clockwise direction if your intention is to spark growth, such as increasing your wealth. If, however, you want to cut back on expenses, stir the tea in a counterclockwise direction to place limits in matters related to finances.

5. Leave a cup of the tea for the fairies who helped you. They'd also like a sweet treat to go with it, such as cookies, cake, or gingerbread.

6. Store leftover tea in the fridge for future use.

INCANTATION TO GET A RAISE

The earliest spells were most likely spoken ones, intoned by witches and wizards, shamans and sorcerers long before the advent of writing. When you utter a spell aloud, you create a resonance that begins the process of manifestation. Sounds produce vibrations that echo through the cosmic web that connects everything in our universe and create effects in the visible world. Ask a sylph to join you, for these air fairies are involved with communication between the realms. The elves, who are among the few fairies who actually have jobs, can also provide assistance. When you're working with fairies, it's often best to use incantations set to a tune because the fae love music.

What's the Difference Between an Affirmation and an Incantation?

Witches use both affirmations and incantations in spellwork. Affirmations are short, positive phrases that describe your intention. They're stated in the present tense, as if the condition you desire already exists. For example, "I now have more than enough money for everything I need and want." Incantations are affirmations set in verse—the rhyme and rhythm help you remember the statement. For example, "Prosperity / Now comes to me / and I am happy as can be."

You Will Need

- Pen or pencil (optional)
- Your book of shadows (optional)
- A musical instrument (optional)
- Food for the fairies

Directions

1. Compose an incantation that states your intention succinctly. It should rhyme, but don't worry about the eloquence of your poetry. For example, you might say something simple like:

    "I now get a raise / and plenty of praise / the money is good / I receive what I should."

    Your incantation can be as long or short as you need it to be to get your point across.

2. If your incantation is lengthy or complex, you may want to write it down in your book of shadows so you don't forget it. Or, you may decide to include it in your book anyway as one of your collection of magickal "recipes" and experiences.

3. Now, if you like, set the words to music. If you have musical talent, you might compose an entire song. Ask your fairy helper to give you inspiration—you may hear her singing along with you.

4. Ask the sylph to carry your intention to whoever is in charge of giving you a raise. To thank the fairy, leave food outside for her on a rock or tree stump.

5. Sing your incantation often, when you're in the shower, driving your car, preparing dinner, anytime that feels right to you. If you can play an instrument, you may choose to accompany yourself on it.

6. When you receive your raise, show gratitude by making a donation to an organization that's working to protect the environment—the nature fairies will be pleased.

ABUNDANCE MEDITATION

Magick begins in your mind. If you can visualize it, you can bring it into your life—that's what the Law of Attraction is all about: What you focus on, you attract. This meditation is actually a guided daydream in which you imagine yourself enjoying all the riches and pleasures the material world has to offer. The more vivid your visualization, the better. Invite a merrow to join you in this meditation—she loves beautiful things and knows how to acquire them.

You Will Need

- A piece of jewelry for the merrow

Directions

1. Eliminate all distractions. Turn off the TV, your phone, etc. If you live with other people, instruct them not to interrupt you, or put a "do not disturb" sign on your door.

2. Sit in a comfy chair or other place where you feel safe and relaxed. Take a few slow, deep breaths to calm and center your mind.

3. Bring to mind a magnificent mansion, estate, castle, manor, or other residence that has everything you've ever dreamed of in it—and it's yours!

4. Envision yourself arriving at this exquisite home in a chauffeur-driven limo. Observe the wonderful landscaping, the gorgeous gardens, the elegant old trees. Exit the limo and see a doorman open the door to let you into the building.

5. As you enter the foyer, feel a sense of welcome, peace, and happiness. This is where you belong. You have come home.

6. Slowly make your way through each of the rooms on the ground floor of this palatial residence. Visualize clearly the furnishings, the artwork, everything that occupies these rooms. Are they decorated with valuable antiques or au courant designer objets d'art?

7. Bring all your senses into the experience. Do you feel luxurious carpets underfoot? Do you smell exotic flowers? Do you hear musicians playing your favorite songs?

8. Wander freely through all the rooms of the mansion, savoring all the treasures and luxuries they contain. Whatever you desire is here at your fingertips, for your enjoyment.

9. When you feel ready, climb a gracefully curving stairway to the second floor. As you did on the ground floor, explore the beauty and abundance that fill the many rooms on this level. Again, realize that everything is yours, everything exists purely for your pleasure. Anything you can imagine is available to you.

10. Once again, bring all your senses into the meditation. The more vivid your visualization, the better. Run your hands along the luxurious fabrics of the upholstery and drapery. Taste the food and drink that have been delivered by servants for your enjoyment. Listen to music playing in the background.

11. If you feel like it, go on to a third level of the mansion. Repeat the exploration as you've done on the lower two floors.

12. In this meditation, you can go anyplace you like. Does the mansion have a wine cellar? Would you like to walk in the gardens? Is there a stable filled with beautiful horses that you can ride across the countryside? Would you enjoy swimming in the pool or lounging on the patio with friends?

13. Spend as long as you like experiencing the unlimited abundance that the universe offers you. When you feel ready, return to your everyday world. But remember what you've witnessed—this is your potential, what's available to you. Now that you know it exists, you're on your way to acquiring it.

14. Leave the piece of jewelry for the merrow as a thank-you gift for her assistance.

15. Repeat this meditation as often as you like. You can elaborate on it to suit your preferences—no limits exist except those you impose on yourself. Whatever you imagine is within the realm of possibility. Enjoy!

Chapter 8

WORKING WITH FAIRIES FOR SAFETY AND PROTECTION

In earlier times, people sought protection from demons, curses, and malevolent forces as well as from dangerous humans, wild animals, bad weather, and disease. They also feared the fairies. To safeguard themselves, their loved ones, and their property, our ancestors employed a variety of spells such as hanging rowan branches over their doorways, tossing salt over their shoulders, and displaying eye amulets to ward off the "evil eye."

Today, witches usually seek protection from ordinary, physical threats—car accidents, burglars, illness, ruthless competitors, annoying neighbors, financial losses, and so on. However, when you're working with fairies, it's a good idea to protect yourself from their mischief too.

> "I believe in everything until it's disproved. So I believe in fairies, the myths, dragons. It all exists, even if it's in your mind."
>
> JOHN LENNON, musician

FAIRIES FOR SAFETY

Which fairies are the best ones to provide protection for you and your loved ones, your home and property? From which fairies, if any, do you seek protection?

- **BROWNIES:** Invite these domestic helpers to assist you in cleansing the area—physically and psychically—in which you cast spells. Rid the space of unwanted entities and energies before you begin, to prevent them from interfering with your work.

- **LEPRECHAUNS:** Known for their cleverness when it comes to money and valuables, these crafty characters can show you how to protect your finances and to guard against fraud.

- **ANIMAL FAIRIES:** Spirit animals can provide protection, just as their physical counterparts do. Not only guard dogs but fairy bears, bulls, lionesses, wild boars, skunks, and geese can help ward off danger.

- **GOBLINS:** The fairy equivalent of human gangs, these fellows can be mischievous or downright mean. In extreme situations, when you feel threatened by enemies, you can bribe them to protect your person or home—like spirit bodyguards or mercenaries. Some tales say they're not very smart, but others describe them as shrewd. They're greedy, so be prepared to pay for their magickal muscle. Remember, they're also tricky and may turn on you if you offend them.

CLEAR DISRUPTIVE ENERGY FROM YOUR SACRED SPACE

Before you begin a spell or ritual, it's a good idea to clear away anything that might interfere with your work. Discordant energy may cause confusion or make a spell go awry. Ask the brownies or kobolds to assist you. Although you shouldn't expect them to run the vacuum cleaner, they are adept at removing bad vibes.

You Will Need

- A broom or besom
- Sea salt
- A sage wand or stick of sage incense
- Matches or a lighter
- Food and drink for the fairies

Directions

1. With your broom or besom, sweep the area—not only the floor but the air as well—to dislodge "stuck" energy and chase it from your sacred space. As you work, sense the air becoming lighter, fresher, and brighter as you remove the psychic smog.

2. Begin in the easternmost part of the space where you plan to do your spellwork. Sprinkle a bit of sea salt there.

3. Walk in a clockwise direction to the southernmost section of the space, and sprinkle some sea salt there.

4. Do the same thing in the west and north. If you prefer, you can cast a complete circle with salt. This is a good option if you're working outdoors because the salt will mix with the earth and produce a more or less permanent protective circle.

5. Light the sage wand or stick of incense.

6. Waft the fragrant smoke all around the area, until you feel you've removed all the unwanted vibrations. Say aloud:

   "THIS SPACE IS NOW CLEANSED AND CLEARED OF ALL HARMFUL,
   DISRUPTIVE, AND UNBALANCED ENERGIES
   IT IS FILLED WITH DIVINE WHITE LIGHT, LOVE, AND JOY."
   (Or, create an affirmation of your own.)

7. When you've finished, leave an offering of food and drink as a thank-you gift for the brownies.

8. Cleanse your sacred space before every spell or ritual you perform.

PROTECTION AMULET FOR WORKING WITH FAIRIES

Fairies are not fanciful, fun-loving playmates. They are not your friends. Nor will they assist you simply out of the goodness of their hearts. Unless your goal aligns with theirs, they may not agree to work with you. If your objective conflicts with theirs, they might trick, block, or even harm you. Make this protection amulet to safeguard yourself when you're performing magick with the fairies or if you decide to visit the land of the fae.

You Will Need
- A disk of stone, wood, ceramic, or metal
- Black paint or nail polish
- A paintbrush

Directions
1. Around the outside of the disk, paint the alchemical symbols for earth, air, fire, and water. The symbol for earth should be positioned at the top of the disk (12:00 on a clock face), the symbol for air at the right side of the disk (3:00), the symbol for fire at the bottom (6:00), and the symbol for water at the left (9:00).

2. In the center, paint a pentagram (a five-pointed star with a circle around it).

3. Before you begin a spell or ritual, hold the amulet to your heart and envision yourself surrounded by pure white light.

4. Say aloud:

> "This amulet keeps me safe and sound,
> at all times and in all situations, now and always."
> (Or, compose your own protection affirmation.)

5. Wear or hold this amulet whenever you do spellwork or rituals with the fae.

PROTECTION DIAGRAM FOR SPELLCASTING

The same symbols you drew on the protection amulet can safeguard you when you perform any type of spell.

You Will Need

- A piece of paper, cardboard, plywood, or other material, cut into a circle large enough for you to stand in
- A black felt marker

Directions

1. Around the outer part of the circle, draw the alchemical symbols for fire, water, air, and earth.

2. In the center, draw a pentagram (a five-pointed star with a circle around it).

3. Before you begin a spell or ritual, stand in the center of the circle you've drawn and envision yourself surrounded by pure white light.

4. Say aloud:

   "I AM SAFE AND SOUND, AT ALL TIMES AND IN ALL SITUATIONS,
   NOW AND ALWAYS."
   (Or, compose your own protection affirmation.)

5. Then proceed with your spell or ritual.

SPELL FOR A SAFE JOURNEY

Although fairies can go anywhere they please in the blink of an eye, and travel freely between our world and their own, we don't read much in folklore about fairies taking trips to and from faraway countries. Chinese fairies don't tend to vacation in Ireland, for instance, nor do Italian fairies turn up in Mexican legends. Elves, however, appear to have migrated from Scandinavia to Britain, and German kobolds bear similarities to Celtic brownies. African fairies are said to have accompanied their people to the Americas during the diaspora.

Nonetheless, you can ask elemental spirits to accompany you and keep you safe the next time you take a trip. If you're traveling by air, seek protection from the sylphs. If you're going on a cruise, request aid from the undines. Few people go long distances on horseback these days, but should you take a trip via equine, a pixie would enjoy riding along with you. Be on the watch, though, because these fairies are notorious horse thieves.

Baba Yaga

Perhaps the strangest mode of transportation belongs to a Russian forest fairy named Baba Yaga, whose story parallels that of the wicked witch in the fairy tale "Hansel and Gretel." Folklore says she paddled around the woods in a mortar and pestle, in which she also pounded herbal medicines and ground the bones of her victims.

You Will Need

- A picture or other likeness of your mode of travel: a photo of a yacht, a toy airplane or car, etc.
- Basil essential oil
- 9 small clear quartz crystals

Directions

1. Place the picture or other likeness of your mode of travel on your altar or another surface where you're performing your spell.

2. Pour a few drops of oil into your palm.

3. Dot a little oil on eight of the quartz crystals.

4. Position the eight crystals in a circle around the image of the mode of transportation you'll take on your trip. Begin at the 9:00 position and set the crystals in place, moving in a clockwise direction until you've completed the circle.

5. Envision a sphere of pure white light surrounding you and the altar.

6. Sense a fairy guardian nearby, as you say this incantation aloud (or compose your own):

"As I travel far and wide
Fairy helper be my guide.
Keep me safe both night and day
And bring me home on [the day you plan to return]."

7. Pick up the eight crystals. Leave the ninth one as a gift for the fairy.

8. Leave the symbol of transportation on your altar until you're ready to depart on your trip. Then pack it, along with one of the crystals from the circle, in your bag to ensure a safe, pleasant journey.

CANDLE SPELL TO PROTECT YOUR HOME

Invite the fire spirits, sometimes called salamanders, to assist you in this spell to safeguard your home—they can be fierce protectors.

"Salamanders are the little ethereal creatures who animate the flame of a hearthfire or candle. They will help you achieve your fiery goals, and they will defend you as well."

NANCY B. WATSON, *Practical Solitary Magic*

You Will Need

- 4 black candles
- An athame, ballpoint pen, nail, nail file, or other sharp object
- Basil essential oil
- 4 candleholders
- Matches or a lighter
- A carnelian

Directions

1. On each candle, inscribe the word SAFE with your sharp object.

2. Pour a little oil into your palm and rub some on each candle to anoint it with protective energy.

3. Fit the candles into the candleholders.

4. Set one candle in the easternmost part of your home, in a place where it can burn safely.

5. Set the second candle in the southernmost part of your home, in a place where it can burn safely.

6. Set the third candle in the westernmost part of your home, in a place where it can burn safely.

7. Set the fourth candle in the northernmost part of your home, in a place where it can burn safely.

8. Go to the eastern part of your home and light the first candle. As you do, say aloud:

> "MY HOME IS SAFE AT ALL TIMES AND IN ALL SITUATIONS,
> NOW AND ALWAYS."
> (Or, compose your own affirmation.)

9. Go to the southern, then the western, and finally the northern part of your home and light the candles positioned there. Repeat the protection affirmation each time you light a candle.

10. You may sense the presence of the fire fairies around you—you might even see them dancing in the flickering candle flames.

11. Allow the candles to burn for at least 10 minutes. Do not leave burning candles unattended.

12. When you feel the spell is working, extinguish the candles. Start at the east and move counterclockwise, extinguishing the candles one by one.

13. Leave the carnelian as a thank-you gift for the fire fairies.

AMBER PROTECTION AMULET

Witches consider amber an agent for protection against physical and nonphysical threats. Of course, amber isn't really a gem; it's a resin. Because it is associated with the fire element, ask the fire spirits to afford you their protection.

You Will Need

- 10 pieces of tumbled golden amber (don't use amber beads with holes in them; drilling holes in gemstones or crystals can kill them)
- A black drawstring pouch
- Amber-scented incense in a holder
- Matches or a lighter

Directions

1. After washing them with mild soap and water, pat nine of the amber pieces dry, slip them into the pouch, and tie it closed. Amber comes in several colors, but for this spell use golden amber—its color is akin to that of fire and the sun. Nine is the number of completion. Witches often use the number three to finalize a spell, and nine is a multiple: three times three.

2. Set the incense in its holder on your altar or another safe place, and light it.

3. Hold the pouch in the incense smoke to charge it.

4. Say aloud:

   "THIS AMULET KEEPS ME SAFE AND SOUND AT ALL TIMES AND IN ALL SITUATIONS, NOW AND ALWAYS."
   (Or, compose your own affirmation.)

5. Allow the incense to finish burning. You may sense or see the fire spirits nearby, maybe in the incense smoke.

6. Leave the tenth piece of amber on your altar as a thank-you gift for the fire fairies.

7. Carry the amber amulet with you to keep you safe.

HERBAL PROTECTION CHARM

Herbal spells are among the most popular ones witches perform—and have been since ancient times, when many witches were also herbalists. Pixies and other earth spirits, who take care of the plant world, can assist you in making this simple but effective protection charm.

You Will Need

- Black paint or a black marker
- A small box, such as a matchbox
- A white or silver pentagram
- Dried basil leaves
- Fennel seeds
- Dried rosemary
- Dried comfrey
- Garlic powder
- Matches or a lighter
- A sage wand or stick of sage incense
- Cookies, milk and honey, or other food for the fairies

Directions

1. With the paint or black marker, completely cover over any pictures, words, or other markings on the box, until the box is totally black.

2. Affix the pentagram to the top of the box. The pentagram may be a sticker, a picture downloaded from the Internet, a small metal milagro (a good luck charm popular in the American Southwest and Mexico, usually little tin images that have symbolic meanings, like the ones people wear on charm bracelets), or one you draw/paint on the box yourself.

3. Put the herbs in the box. Shake it three times to combine the ingredients.

4. Light the sage wand or incense. Hold the box in the smoke to charge the charm.

5. Say aloud:

"THIS MAGICK CHARM PROTECTS ME AT ALL TIMES
AND IN ALL SITUATIONS, ALWAYS AND ALL WAYS."
(Or, compose your own affirmation.)

6. Leave the food and/or drink outdoors as a thank-you gift for the nature fairies.

7. Carry the protection charm with you at all times to keep you safe wherever you go. You may want to make these simple, inexpensive charms for friends, family members, and other loved ones too.

CREATE A PROTECTION MANDALA FOR YOUR HOME

Mandala is a Sanskrit word for a diagram—usually circular or square—that contains images of deities and/or symbols of a spiritual or magickal nature. It represents the universe and is often used as an aid to meditation. This one, however, provides protection from unwanted beings, physical or nonphysical. Because it includes images of all four elements, you may want to solicit the spirits of the air, earth, fire, and water to participate in the mandala's creation.

You Will Need

- A piece of construction paper, cardboard, plywood, cloth, or other material
- Markers or paint of various colors that are appropriate for use on whatever material you've chosen
- Food for the fairies

Directions

1. Lay the piece of paper, cardboard, or other material—it can be any size you choose—on a table or work area. You can work on your altar, if you like.

2. Draw or paint a circle that represents the universe. To witches, a circle also symbolizes protection.

3. Inside the circle, draw or paint a square to represent the earth. The corners of the square should touch the circle.

4. In the center of the square, draw or paint a pentagram.

5. In each of the corners of the square, draw or paint a symbol of one of the four elements. If you're feeling especially creative or have artistic talent, you might prefer to illustrate the corners with pictures of the zodiac animal signs for the four elements: the bull, lion, eagle, and human water bearer. You can see these symbols on The World card in the tarot.

6. Add whatever images represent safety and protection to you. These may be pictures as lofty as a guardian angel or as mundane as an umbrella. For example, if you're a sailor, you could draw the goddess Quan Yin (who protects seafarers) or a lifesaver. Don't think you have to be a Michelangelo to succeed with this spell; your sincerity and intention are what count.

7. Enjoy the process. You may sense the fairies in your presence, having fun expressing their creativity and lending their magick to your spell.

8. When you've finished, display your mandala in a place where you'll see it often. If you've made it from material that can withstand the weather, you might choose to hang it outside on your home like the hex signs we associate with the Pennsylvania Dutch.

9. Say aloud:

> "PROTECT THIS HOME,
> HIGH TO LOW,
> FENCE TO FENCE,
> DOOR TO DOOR,
> LIGHT TO DENSE,
> ROOF TO FLOOR."

10. Leave food as a thank-you gift for the fairies.

ASK A DRAGON TO BE YOUR GUARDIAN

Spirit animals come in many shapes, some of them mythological, such as dragons or unicorns. Shapeshifting fairies like to transform themselves into animals, birds, and other creatures, as many legends and fairy tales tell us—the story of Cerridwen and Gwion in Chapter 3 is a good example. Of all the magickal beasts in lore and legends, dragons continue to be among the most fascinating to us. In China, dragons are said to bring good luck. In this spell, you tap their ferocious nature to protect you from enemies and danger of all kinds.

> "Above us, outlined against the brilliant sky, dragons crowded every available perching space on the Rim. And the sun made a gold of every one of them."
>
> ANNE MCCAFFREY, *Nerilka's Story*

You Will Need

- An image of a dragon
- Dragon's blood incense in an incense holder
- Matches or a lighter
- White snapdragons

Directions

1. Find an image of a dragon from a magazine or book, downloaded from the Internet, or a small figurine of one.

2. Set the image on your altar or other flat surface.

3. Set the incense in its holder beside the image of the dragon.

4. Light the incense, and as the smoke drifts up to the spirit world, imagine it reaching a dragon that will serve as your guardian. Ask the dragon to protect you and sense it agreeing.

5. Leave the snapdragons in a vase on your altar, or put them outside as a thank-you gift for the spirit dragon.

6. Carry the image of the dragon with you to keep you safe.

PROTECTION POTION FOR YOUR PET

Pretty snowflake obsidian combines black and white, two colors that witches associate with protection. It safeguards against both physical and nonphysical threats. Put a few drops of this potion in your pet's food or water each day to provide protection. If you like, you can also rub a little on its collar.

You Will Need

- A glass jar with a lid
- 1 piece of snowflake obsidian
- Scissors
- A piece of paper
- A pen, pencil, marker, or crayon
- Tape
- Water
- Food for the fairy animal

Directions

1. Ask a spirit animal to serve as your pet's guardian. The fairy animal may be of the same species as your pet (though nonphysical) or another one that agrees to help. An iguana might even volunteer to guard a goat—any combination is possible. That's because in the spirit realm we don't see one another as adversaries, as predators and prey.

2. Wash the jar and the obsidian with mild soap and water.

3. Cut the paper to make a label that you'll affix to the jar.

4. Draw a pentagram on the label and tape it to the jar, with the image of the pentagram facing in. The protective energy of the pentagram will imprint the water.

5. Put the obsidian in the jar.

6. Add water, put the lid on the jar, and shake it gently three times to charge the potion.

7. Leave food for the animal fairy as a thank-you gift.

8. Replenish your pet's water bowl at least once each day with fresh water, and add a little of this magick potion to provide ongoing protection.

FLORAL PROTECTION FOR YOUR HOME

Flowers have magickal powers, just like herbs and other plants do. Usually, white flowers are considered the best ones to use for overall protection. Carnations provide strength and endurance. White lilacs banish negative energy. Lilies shield you against hexes and negative vibes coming from other people. Snapdragons guard against deception. You can find plenty of additional information online or in books about the meanings of flowers.

You Will Need

- Fresh-cut flowers or live plants
- A vase
- Water
- Food for the fairies

Directions

1. Ask the pixies and other nature spirits, who serve as caretakers for the plant world, to assist you. Put a bouquet of fresh-cut flowers or plants in a vase (a black vase is best, as black is a color witches connect with protection) with water and set it near the front door. If you prefer, plant live flowers outside your home—or do both. You can put flowers in every room of your home, if you like.

2. As soon as you notice the petals starting to wilt, replace the flowers with fresh ones.

3. Remember to leave food for the fairies to thank them for their aid—pixies like cookies and other sweets, as well as milk and honey.

SPELL TO DEFLECT BAD VIBES

This spell protects your home by sending bad vibes of all kinds back to their source. Use it to repel disruptive energy from humans or spirits. If your goal is to safeguard your home from a person or persons, and you have solicited aid from the fairies, make sure to leave food for them as a thank-you gift.

You Will Need

- 1 or more mirrors
- Food for the fairies

Directions

1. Any size or shape mirror will do, but an octagon-shaped mirror, which feng shui practitioners consider fortunate, is best, if you can find one.

2. Hang the mirrors in a window located in the direction of the disruption. The reflective side of the mirror should face out, toward the source of the problem. If you sense the bad vibes are coming from more than one direction, hang a mirror in each window you associate with unpleasant energy.

3. When harmful vibes are directed at you, the mirror(s) will bounce the energy back to whoever or whatever generated it.

4. Leave the mirror(s) in place until you feel certain you are no longer the target of unwanted energy.

5. Leave food for the fairies to thank them for their assistance.

PROTECT YOURSELF WITH PINE, PART ONE

Witches associate pine with cleansing and protection. This spell has two parts: The first one keeps you safe, and the second protects your home or place of business. Ask the pixies, who take care of trees and the plant kingdom, to assist you.

You Will Need

- A cauldron, barbecue grill, fireplace, or other place in which to safely build a fire
- A piece of pine or pine chips
- Matches or a lighter
- A black pouch, preferably one made of silk
- A piece of white ribbon 6 inches long
- Food for the fairies

Directions

1. In the cauldron, grill, or fireplace, place the pine or pine chips.

2. Light the wood and let it burn completely. (Caution: Don't leave a burning fire unattended.)

3. When the ashes have cooled, scoop some into the pouch. Save the remaining ashes for Part Two of this spell.

4. With the white ribbon, make eight knots to tie the pouch closed. As you tie each knot, say aloud:

   "THIS AMULET KEEPS ME SAFE AT ALL TIMES AND IN ALL SITUATIONS, NOW AND ALWAYS."

   If you're making the amulet for someone else, substitute that person's name for "me."

5. Leave food for the pixies to thank them for their assistance.

6. Carry the pouch with you for protection, or give it to the person you made it for.

PROTECT YOURSELF WITH PINE, PART TWO

In this part of the pine protection spell, you begin by tapping into the wood's cleansing and purification properties. Again, ask the pixies and other nature spirits for their help.

You Will Need

- Pine incense
- An incense holder
- Matches or a lighter
- Ashes left over from Part One of this spell
- A bowl or other container
- Food for the fairies

Directions

1. Fit the incense into the holder and light it.

2. Walk through all the rooms of your home or place of business, letting the fragrant smoke cleanse and clear the space of harmful, disruptive, or imbalanced energies.

3. You can also cleanse your car this way by allowing the pine smoke to waft about in the car's interior.

4. When you've finished, put the ashes from Part One in a bowl or other open container.

5. Dip your finger in the ashes, and then draw a pentagram on the outside of each door of your home or place of business with the ashes. It doesn't matter that the ashes will soon blow or wash away—the spell is cast, and its energy remains long after the ashes have disappeared.

6. Do the same with your car. Draw a pentagram with ashes on the front and back bumpers.

7. As you work, envision your home, place of business, or car surrounded by pure white light, providing protection at all times and in all situations.

8. Leave food for the fairies to thank them for assisting you.

PROTECTION APPLE PIE

Did you know that apples not only have healthful properties, but they also contain a secret source of protection? Cut one in half, and you'll notice the seeds form a pentagram inside. Use organic ingredients, if possible, to make this magick apple pie—you'll win points with the nature fairies for eschewing pesticides.

You Will Need

- 2 (9-inch) piecrusts
- A pie pan
- Measuring cups and spoons
- 2 bowls
- ⅓ cup granulated sugar
- ⅓ cup brown sugar
- 1 tablespoon flour
- ½ teaspoon cinnamon
- ¼ teaspoon nutmeg
- ⅛ teaspoon salt
- A knife
- 6 or so medium-sized tart apples
- 3 tablespoons butter
- A fork

Directions

1. Preheat oven to 425°F.

2. Place one of the piecrusts in the pie pan.

3. In one bowl, combine the sugars, flour, and spices.

4. Cut the apples in half. Take a moment to reflect on the pentagram of seeds inside each apple and the meaning of the pentagram as a symbol of protection, before removing the seeds. (Note: Save the seeds for other spells.)

5. Cut the apples into slices and lay half of them in the piecrust.

6. Sprinkle the apples with half the sugar mixture, then dot with pats of butter.

7. Arrange the rest of the apple slices on top of the first layer; sprinkle with the remaining sugar mixture and pats of butter.

8. Place the second piecrust over the apples and pinch together the edges to seal the two crusts around the fruit.

9. With the fork, poke holes in the shape of a pentagram in the center of the top crust.

10. Bake for about 40–50 minutes, until the crust is golden brown. (You may need to cover the pie with aluminum foil toward the end to keep the crust from burning.)

11. Serve the pie warm to friends and loved ones—and, of course, offer some to the fairies who love sweets.

Mythical Apples

Apples figure prominently in many myths, most famously in the Genesis account of the Garden of Eden. The story usually describes Eve's offering of the apple from the Tree of Knowledge to Adam in dark, pejorative terms. However, my interpretation is that the seeds in the apple, arranged in the shape of a pentagram that represents the five points of the human body, symbolize Adam and Eve assuming corporeal bodies and coming to live on earth as human beings.

Other famous myths about apples include the Greek story of the Judgment of Paris, in which Paris of Troy had to judge a divine beauty contest and decide which of three gorgeous goddesses—Athena, Aphrodite, and Hera—was the loveliest. The prize was a golden apple. His choice led to the Trojan War. Then, of course, there's the magickal Isle of Avalon in the Arthurian legends, where beautiful apples grew year-round and scented the entire island. The word *avalon* bears similarities to various Celtic terms for "apple." Hidden in the mists, Avalon is believed to be home to the fairies and the most famous fairy witch of all: Morgan le Fay.

SEAL OF SAFETY

In days of old, people used sealing wax to close letters. Often the sender impressed the wax with a personal stamp while the wax was still warm, to let the recipient know who had written the letter. In this spell, you write a letter to yourself to reinforce the belief that you are safe, secure, courageous, protected by higher forces, and so on. Fire spirits could be suitable allies when working this spell; however, tune in to your intuition and see which members of the fae come forward to say they'd like to work with you.

You Will Need

- 1 black candle
- 1 white candle
- Rosemary essential oil
- 2 candleholders
- Matches or a lighter
- A piece of paper
- A pen, pencil, marker, or other writing tool
- An envelope
- A toothpick
- Food for the fairies

Directions

1. Dress both candles with the oil. Pour a little oil in your palms and rub a thin coat on the candles to anoint them, but not on the wicks.

2. Fit the candles into holders so they can burn safely.

3. Set the black candle on your altar at your right, and the white one at your left. If you don't have an altar, position the candles this way on a table or other surface. Light the candles.

4. On the piece of paper, by candlelight, write a letter to yourself describing how brave, strong, self-confident, daring, etc. you are. Also state that you are safe and sound, comfortable and secure, protected by divine guides and guardians at all times and in all situations. Make sure to word the letter in a positive way, and in the present tense as if the protection you seek is already yours. It can be as long or as short, as detailed or as simple as you want it to be.

5. When you've said everything you want to say, fold the paper and slip it into the envelope.

6. Drip a little melted wax from each candle on the envelope's flap to seal it.

7. When the wax has cooled somewhat but is still soft, use the toothpick to inscribe your initials or a symbol that has meaning for you, such as a pentagram, in the wax.

8. If you've chosen to work with the fae in this spell, leave food for them as a thank-you gift.

9. Carry the letter with you, put it under your pillow at night, or display it in a place where you'll see it often.

KNOT SPELL TO BIND AN ENEMY

This spell uses sympathetic magick to prevent someone from harming you, your loved ones, property, etc. Instead of binding the actual person physically, you fashion an effigy that represents your adversary and then use symbolism to accomplish your objective. Ask the fae which of them may be willing to assist you. Fire spirits can be enthusiastic allies. In extreme cases, you might turn to the pookas or members of the Unseelie Court for help, but they can be difficult to control and may be destructive. If you decide to work with these fairies, make sure to negotiate terms and conditions carefully before you begin.

You Will Need
- A small figurine made of wax, wood, cloth, clay, or straw
- A blank, self-stick label or piece of masking tape
- A felt-tip marker or pen
- Biodegradable string
- A shovel
- A large rock
- A thank-you gift or other payment for the fairies

Directions
1. Fashion a figure, also known by witches as a poppet, to represent the person who seeks to do you harm.

2. On the label or tape, write the full name of the person. Affix it to the effigy you've fashioned. It is now a symbol for your enemy, and whatever you do to it has an effect on the person it represents.

3. Tie the poppet's hands and feet with the string, then wrap string around its entire body. As you tie knots, say aloud:

> "I BIND YOU TIGHTLY AS CAN BE /
> YOU HAVE NO POWER OVER ME /
> WHAT ILL YOU DO RETURNS TO THEE."

(Or, compose your own incantation.)

4. When you're confident that you've immobilized your enemy, take the poppet to a place far from your home. This should be a spot away from trees or water.

5. Dig a hole in the ground and put the effigy in it. Cover it with dirt, and then place the stone on top of the burial spot.

6. Leave whatever thank-you payment you've agreed to for the fairies who participated in your spell.

SHAPESHIFT FOR SAFETY

This practice lets you tap in to the power of an animal fairy to provide protection. No, you won't actually transform into the animal. Instead, you call up its energy and let it temporarily infuse you with strength, speed, courage, dexterity—whatever traits you need to safeguard yourself in a particular situation.

You Will Need

- Food for the spirit animal

Directions

1. Decide which animal possesses the characteristics you need. For example, a bear has great strength and can be fierce when threatened. Cheetahs have exceptional speed. Foxes are known for their cleverness.

2. Take a few minutes to connect with that animal in spirit. In your mind's eye, examine and admire the animal's qualities. Then ask the animal to lend you its powers temporarily. Wait until you feel it agree to help you.

3. Assume a pose that resembles the animal's when it is either defending itself or attacking an adversary. If you're shapeshifting to a gorilla, beat your chest with your hands. If you're taking on the energy of a lion, bare your teeth and growl. Continue doing this, even though you may feel a bit silly at first.

4. Invite the animal's energy to flow into you. Feel what it might be like to actually *be* that creature. Envision yourself and the animal merging, becoming allies, becoming one in spirit.

5. As the animal's power enhances your own, bring to mind the situation, person, or challenge with which you seek help.

6. Sense yourself wielding the powers of the spirit animal. What would it do in this circumstance? Allow the animal's instincts to guide your actions.

7. Revel in your confidence and fearlessness. Know that you have the ability to accomplish your goal. See yourself triumphing over the obstacles or adversaries that have frightened or blocked you in the past. Imagine those problems dissolving, running away, growing small and insignificant.

8. Continue in this manner for as long as you want. When you feel you've accomplished what you set out to do, gradually sense yourself separating from the spirit animal and return fully to your human self.

9. Set out food to thank the spirit animal for its help.

ST· JOHN'S WORT PROTECTION POTION

Folklore tells us that the herb called St. John's wort repels fairies—maybe they don't like it because it's named for a Christian saint. If a fairy (or more than one) is bothering you and you'd rather it left you alone, make this protection potion. You can purchase St. John's wort in health food stores, supermarkets, or any place you'd buy vitamins and other supplements. Caution: This herb may interact adversely with some medications, such as antidepressants. Although you'll only be using a tiny bit, check to make sure it's safe for you.

You Will Need
- A clear glass bottle or jar with a lid
- 4 ounces of water
- 1 tablet or capsule of St. John's wort

Directions

1. Wash the bottle or jar with mild soap and water.

2. Pour in the water.

3. Add the St. John's wort.

4. Put the lid on the bottle or jar and shake three times to charge the potion. Let the potion sit until the St. John's wort dissolves completely.

5. Dip your finger in the potion and draw a pentagram with it on your heart center. If you prefer not to put the potion directly on your skin, pour a little on a handkerchief and carry it in your pocket to repel the fairy.

6. Say aloud:

> "Fairy go and leave me be /
> I'll not harm you and don't harm me."
> (Or, compose your own statement.)

7. Make more batches of this potion as needed.

IRON AMULET TO REPEL A FAIRY

Here's another way to ward off a troublesome fairy. According to legends, fairies don't like iron—which may be why people hang iron horseshoes above their doorways. You'll need one of these amulets for each exterior door.

You Will Need

- 3 iron nails
- A square of black cloth about 3 inches by 3 inches
- A white ribbon

Directions

1. Lay the nails on the piece of cloth, alternating the nail heads so that two point in one direction and the one in the middle points in the opposite direction.

2. Fold the cloth around the nails.

3. Tie the ribbon around the packet, making three knots. Each time you tie a knot, say aloud:

> "FAIRY GO AND LEAVE ME BE /
> I'LL NOT HARM YOU AND DON'T HARM ME."
> (Or, compose your own statement.)

4. Place an amulet just outside each door to your home, under the welcome mat, beside the step, or in another inconspicuous spot. Or, tie it on a doorknob.

Chapter 9

WORKING WITH FAIRIES FOR HEALTH AND HEALING

Since ancient times, witches have engaged in the healing arts as midwives, cunning folk, and herbalists. People sought their aid for emotional and spiritual ills, for protecting crops and livestock, and for rectifying upsets in the land. Many contemporary witches are healers too, following in our ancestors' footsteps. We're still midwives and herbalists, as well as massage therapists, aromatherapists, naturopaths, crystal workers, sound healers, homeopaths, Reiki practitioners—even MDs, opticians, and dentists.

Fairies also have a long history as healers who use their powers in both the physical and nonphysical worlds. Morgan le Fay was considered a gifted healer, as well as a witch and a fairy. The Celtic goddess Aine, who's sometimes thought of in Ireland as the Fairy Queen, was revered as a healer deity—the water in her lake, Lough Gur, reputedly offers medicinal benefits to those who immerse themselves in it. Today the fae may be willing to collaborate with witches as they once did in order to bring about health and well-being to all of earth's inhabitants as well as to the planet itself.

Please be advised that the spells, rituals, and concoctions included in this chapter are not intended to be a substitute for professional medical treatment. If you have a health concern, it's always wise to seek the care and advice of a trained, qualified physician. Magickal and spiritual healing, however, can serve as valuable assets to modern medical procedures and therapies.

HEALING AND THE FAE

Which fairies can increase your healing knowledge and skills? Which can show you how to formulate potions, poultices, salves, teas, and other magickal concoctions for health and healing?

- **PIXIES:** These nature spirits are respected for their vast knowledge of plant magick. Because they care for, nurture, and protect the world's botanicals, they understand the medicinal power of plants and know which ones to use as remedies.

- **ELVES:** In addition to being skilled artisans and craftspeople, elves are admired in the fairy world as talented healers. These hardworking and diligent folk can also serve as fairy personal trainers. They'll help you develop an exercise routine—and stick to it.

- **MERROWS:** Folklore tells us these beautiful water spirits sometimes mate with human beings. Because they don't experience romantic feelings or commit themselves to a single partner—nor do they believe in everlasting love—they can help you heal from a broken heart or another type of emotional disappointment.

- *BEAN SIDHES:* According to legends, these fairies notify families when one of their members is about to pass into the spirit realm. They move between the manifest and spirit worlds—what we think of as the worlds of the "living" and the "dead"—and they know that our spirits live on after our bodies die. Therefore, they can help people deal with grief over the loss of a loved one or ease the fear of their own imminent deaths.

OGHAM PRAYER FLAG BLESSING TO HEAL THE WORLD

Buddhists hang prayer flags outside their homes, temples, and other places to send blessings around the world. On colored squares of cloth, they draw pictures and write prayers, then tie the flags on lengths of rope and hang them where the flags will flutter in the breeze. The wind carries the intentions illustrated on the flags to all beings everywhere. You, too, can employ this lovely tradition to bring healing to the world. Instead of Buddhist imagery, write blessings in your own language and/or draw symbols that convey your intentions. If you like, you can draw the Ogham glyph for ivy (*gort*), which, according to Druid tradition, nourishes hungry animals and encourages rebirth after times of destruction, such as wildfires or earthquakes. Invite the sylphs, the fairies of the air, to fly your prayers to the four corners of the earth.

You Will Need

- Squares of cloth, as many as you like, in whatever colors you prefer
- Felt-tip marker(s)
- A length of rope or string
- Staples, thread, safety pins, or something else with which to affix the flags to the rope
- Incense
- Matches or a lighter

Directions

1. Cut pieces of cloth in a size that's convenient for you to work with, about a 6- to 12-inch square. Choose the seven colors of the rainbow or colors that appeal to you.

2. On the flags, write your intentions: to slow global warming, to bring rain to a drought-plagued region, to prevent and clean up oil spills and other forms of pollution, to increase human beings' awareness of our role in caring for the earth. As you work, focus your mind on your intention and envision it manifesting in the physical world.

3. When you've finished, fasten the flags to the rope using whatever method you've chosen.

4. Take the flags outside and hang them in a place where the wind will catch them. You may want to tie them on a fence, a tree, a porch railing, or a flagpole.

5. Invite the sylphs to assist you by ferrying your blessings to those for whom they're intended. You may notice sparks of light flickering around you, like fireflies, which indicates the fairies' willingness to participate.

6. Thank the fairies and burn incense in their honor to show your appreciation.

7. When the flags begin to fade or fray, replace them.

Ancient Books of Healing Magick

One of the earliest and most influential grimoires (a.k.a. books of shadows), *Clavicula Salomonis* or *Key of Solomon*, was supposedly written by the great King Solomon and believed to have appeared in the Middle East some two thousand years ago. By the fifteenth century, the book had found its way into the hands of European scholars and others who sought to learn the secrets of the wise king. Among the many spells included in the book were those for dealing with various types of spirits. Another ancient spell book, the *Sefer HaRazim*, which Noah is said to have passed down to King Solomon, contained techniques for healing as well as for divination and attracting good fortune.

RITUAL TO STRENGTHEN VITALITY

Often we think of fairies wielding magick wands to make someone disappear or to transform one thing into something else. Witches, however, use wands to direct energy. The wand also represents the fire element, which energizes and stimulates physical vitality. In this ritual you use your wand to draw upon the powers of heaven and earth to strengthen your immune system and your body's innate ability to ward off illness. Ask an elf to assist you—elves possess great strength and keen healing powers. You can perform this ritual for another person too.

Healing Spells for Other People

Before you do a healing spell for another person, ask that person's permission. Although your goal may be well intended, you might not know the reason that individual is sick. Sometimes illness has a beneficial purpose; for example, if someone has been working too hard, coming down with a cold or flu could provide a few days of needed rest. If the person isn't able to answer you directly, you can send your question mentally and wait to receive a response. Let your intuition guide you.

You Will Need

- A magick wand
- Food for the elf

Directions

1. Stand with your feet about shoulder-width apart. You may sense the elf standing near you.

2. Hold the wand over your head with both hands, arms outstretched and straight, pointing the tip of the wand at the sky.

3. Say aloud:

> "WITH THIS WAND I DRAW DOWN STRENGTH, VITALITY,
> AND HEALING ENERGY FROM THE HEAVENS."

   In your mind's eye see light flowing into the wand, filling it with cosmic energy and making it glow brightly. You may sense the wand tingling or growing warmer.

4. Visualize the energy you've collected with the wand now streaming into your body, filling you with vitality. You may feel stronger, more alive, more powerful.

5. When you sense that all the light has been transferred from the wand into your body, point the wand at the ground.

6. Say aloud:

> "WITH THIS WAND I DRAW UP THE NURTURING, SUPPORTIVE,
> HEALING FORCE OF MOTHER EARTH."

   In your mind's eye see light flowing into the wand from the center of the earth, filling the wand and making it glow brightly. Perhaps you'll sense the wand resonating with nourishing energy or hear a faint humming sound.

7. Envision the light you've collected from the earth flowing into your body, feeding and strengthening you.

8. When you sense that all the light has been transferred from the wand into your body, envision the two forces, heavenly and earthly, blending within you. Visualize them swirling together from your

feet up to the top of your head and back down to your feet again. Feel this powerful mix enlivening and vitalizing every cell, every nerve, every fiber.

9. Enjoy this sensation for as long as you like. When you've finished, set out food for the elf as a thank-you gift.

10. Repeat this ritual whenever you feel a need for an energy boost or want to reinforce your body's natural ability to resist potential illness.

> "Throughout the history of medicine, including the shamanic healing traditions, the Greek tradition of Asclepius, Aristotle and Hippocrates, and the folk and religious healers, the imagination has been used to diagnose disease."
>
> JEANNE ACHTERBERG, *Imagery in Healing: Shamanism and Modern Medicine*

RITUAL BATH FOR RELAXATION

Nearly three thousand years ago, Greek physician Hippocrates, known as the "father of medicine," recommended enjoying a daily bath and an aromatic massage to maintain optimal health. Bathing in Epsom salts, Dead Sea salts, or pink Himalayan salts will provide relaxation and bring relief from aches by drawing toxins out of your body. Witches also take ritual baths prior to spellcasting because doing so calms the mind, washes away daily stress, and shifts your awareness from mundane to magickal. Invite the water fairies called undines to join you.

You Will Need
- 1 cup of Epsom salts, Dead Sea salts, or pink Himalayan bath salts
- Several drops of lavender essential oil
- 4 amethyst crystals
- 1 or more candles in candleholders
- Matches or a lighter
- Soothing music

Directions

1. Run a tub of comfortably hot water and add the bath salts to the water.

2. Add the essential oil, in whatever amount smells good to you.

3. Set one amethyst crystal at each corner of your bathtub.

4. Position the candle(s) where it/they can burn safely, then turn off the overhead lights.

5. Play soothing music on your phone or other device. Fairies love music and will be happy to join you in this relaxing ritual. You may notice the surface of the water rippling or see flattish bubbles forming on it—that's a sign the undines are present.

6. Soak into the tub, letting the pleasantly hot water wash away stress, minor aches, and worries. Notice how the aroma of the lavender essential oil calms your mind. Feel the amethysts gently shifting you out of your ordinary thinking and into a higher level of spiritual awareness. Allow this peaceful environment to dissolve your troubles, at least for the time being.

7. Sense the undines playing around you in the water. Take a cue from these spirits, who float above anxiety and swim easily through troubled waters. Ask them to teach you to balance your emotions and release stress, so that you move gracefully and joyfully through life.

8. Spend as long as you like in your ritual bath. When you've finished, extinguish the candles. Empty the tub and turn off the music.

9. Dot one of the amethysts with essential oil and leave it for the undines.

10. You may not be able to enjoy this magickal experience every day, as Hippocrates recommended, but you should try to pamper yourself as often as possible.

BREW HERBAL TEA TO IMPROVE DIGESTION

Throughout history, witches have served as the medicine women and men in their communities. Long before we had the benefits of modern medical procedures and pharmaceuticals, these healers relied on herbs along with massage, acupressure, and other natural therapies—including potions, oils, poultices, gem elixirs, and magick remedies—to facilitate wellness. Herbal teas are among the oldest and most widely used aids to good health. Pixies and other nature fairies, who have extensive knowledge of the plant world, can help you concoct and empower this soothing beverage by infusing it with their wisdom.

> "A healer's power stems not from any special ability, but from maintaining the courage and awareness to embody and express the universal healing power that every human being naturally possesses."
>
> ERIC MICHA'EL LEVENTHAL, author

You Will Need

- 12 ounces of hot water
- A teapot
- Chamomile, loose tea or a tea bag
- Peppermint, loose tea or a tea bag
- Ginger, loose tea or a tea bag
- A ceramic or glass cup with no designs or words on it
- Lemon juice to taste
- Honey to taste
- A spoon, preferably silver or silverplate
- Food for the fairies

Directions

1. After heating the water to boiling, pour a little into the teapot. Swirl it around to warm the pot, then dump out the water and pour the rest of the water into the teapot.

2. Add the loose herbs or tea bags to the pot and let them steep until the brew is as strong as you like it.

3. Sense the fairies adding their magick touch to the brew. After several minutes, strain out the herbs or remove the tea bags.

4. Pour the tea into your cup. Add the lemon juice and honey, in whatever amounts taste good to you. With your spoon, stir in a clockwise direction to attract healing benefits, or stir in a counter-clockwise direction to dispel nausea or other discomfort.

5. Feel the tea's pleasant warmth and healing herbs calming your distress, gently bringing your digestive system into balance.

6. According to holistic healing concepts, physical illnesses often have corresponding emotional components. Herbert Benson, bestselling author of *The Relaxation Response*, explains that stress is a factor in a majority of ailments—including those that involve the digestive system. While you sip this soothing tea, ask yourself some questions that may reveal clues to the source of your digestive discomfort. For example: *What things in my life am I having trouble digesting? What can't I stomach about a particular situation?*

7. Allow insights to arise into your awareness. Ask the fairies to contribute information that could be useful to you too. They may suggest additional herbs that can benefit you or recommend complementary healing practices.

8. Leave food outside for the fairies who have assisted you to thank them for their help and guidance.

9. Brew this healthful tea regularly and drink it until you experience relief from the digestive problems that troubled you. You may choose to drink it on a daily basis as a preventive measure.

MEDITATE WITH GREEN GEMSTONES FOR EMOTIONAL HEALTH AND WELL-BEING

Crystal healers connect green gemstones with the heart chakra and emotional well-being. You, too, can benefit from working with these stones. Pixies, who care for the earth's resources, can teach you the properties of gemstones and how to use them to generate healing. Elves may also agree to share their healing magick with you.

You Will Need

- 1 piece of tumbled malachite
- 1 piece of tumbled green jade
- 1 piece of green tourmaline
- 1 piece of tumbled green agate
- Your book of shadows
- Food for the fairies

Directions

1. Wash the stones with mild soap and water before you begin working with them.

2. On the first day, sit in a quiet, comfortable place where you won't be disturbed. Silence your phone, the TV, and other distractions.

3. Hold the piece of malachite in your hand while you breathe slowly and deeply. Let your mind relax. Attune yourself to the stone's energy—you may feel it resonating, growing warmer, or something else. Malachite strengthens your spiritual force and enhances beneficial energy by stimulating your immune system. Ancient Egyptian women ground the stone and wore it on their eyelids, not only for cosmetic purposes but also because it helped prevent eye infections.

4. Meditate with the gem for as long as you like. When you finish, thank the stone for its benefits. Write in your book of shadows what you experienced and include any insights you may have received from the fae during your meditation.

5. Leave food outside for the fairies to thank them for their assistance.

6. On the second day, hold the piece of jade in your hand and attune yourself to its energy. Jade promotes spiritual healing, tranquility, and emotional balance. It enhances feelings of being loved and being worthy of love. This gemstone helps you release negative thinking and tension, thereby enabling your body to cleanse itself of toxins. In China, jade has long been considered a stone of good luck.

7. Meditate with the gem for as long as you like. When you finish, thank the stone for its benefits. Write in your book of shadows what you experienced and include any insights you may have received from the fae during your meditation.

8. Leave food outside for the fairies to thank them for their assistance.

9. On the third day, hold the piece of tourmaline in your hand and attune yourself to its energy. Green tourmaline supports heart healing and spiritual strength to elevate positive feelings. It also clears negativity and helps to balance the etheric body, so that disharmony doesn't manifest in physical problems.

10. Meditate with the gem for as long as you like. When you finish, thank the stone for its benefits. Write in your book of shadows what you experienced and include any insights you may have received from the fae during your meditation.

11. Leave food outside for the fairies to thank them for their assistance.

12. On the fourth day, hold the piece of agate in your hand and attune yourself to its energy. Green agate encourages inner harmony and supports healing from emotional traumas. It's also connected with fertility. According to Judy Hall, author of *The Encyclopedia of Crystals*, "In ancient times women would drink water in which a Green Agate had been soaked, to guard against sterility."

13. Meditate with the gem for as long as you like. When you finish, thank the stone for its benefits. Write in your book of shadows what you experienced and include any insights you may have received from the fae during your meditation.

14. Leave food outside for the fairies to thank them for their assistance.

Healing with Crystals and Gemstones

You can use crystals and gemstones to promote healing in a number of ways. Wear them as jewelry or carry them on your person to continually strengthen your aura. Place one on the site of an injury or ailment to attract healing energy and ease discomfort. Set them in your environment to protect against unwanted vibes; for example, by your computer to block EMFs. Combine them with herbs, liquids, and other substances to enhance healing benefits.

CREATE A GEMSTONE TALISMAN FOR BETTER SLEEP

Do you find it difficult to fall asleep or to stay asleep? Are you bothered by unpleasant dreams? When you wake in the morning, do you still feel tired? Lack of sleep can lead to an array of health problems as well as accidents. This talisman draws upon the energies of six gemstones that have been used for centuries to improve rest and relaxation. The pixies and other nature spirits can help you learn about and work with the powers of gemstones.

You Will Need

- 1 piece of tumbled malachite
- 1 piece of jade
- 1 piece of amethyst
- 1 piece of rose quartz
- 1 piece of tumbled labradorite
- 1 piece of tumbled leopardskin jasper
- A dark blue drawstring pouch, preferably made of silk
- Food for the fairies
- Your book of shadows

Directions

1. Wash the stones with mild soap and water before you begin working with them.

   - Malachite eases fears that can cause nightmares, especially in children. Our ancestors also wore it to guard against the "evil eye."
   - Jade encourages insightful and prophetic dreams.
   - The most frequently used gem for relaxation, amethyst calms restless thinking that can disturb sleep and brings feelings of tranquility.
   - Rose quartz soothes and balances the emotions while promoting feelings of love, kindness, and compassion.
   - Labradorite helps you remember your dreams and understand their meanings. It also encourages creative dreaming that can lead to problem-solving during your waking hours.

- Leopardskin jasper protects against negativity and anxiety that can prevent you from relaxing. It also helps you gain inner strength while you sleep.

2. Put all six gemstones in the pouch and tie it closed.

3. Place the pouch under your pillow or on your bedside table at night to help you sleep and dream better.

4. Leave food outside for the fairies to thank them for their assistance.

5. Record your dreams along with insights you've received from them in your book of shadows.

Magickal Dreamcatchers

Consider hanging a dreamcatcher above or beside your bed to bring sweet dreams and help you sleep better. Originally designed by the indigenous people of North America, a dreamcatcher, or "sacred hoop," is usually a circle made of wood with a web or net stretched across it. The web represents the protector deity known as Spider Woman. Feathers, beads, and other decorations may be affixed to the dreamcatcher as well. Willow is a favorite wood for the circle. To witches, the circle symbolizes protection. The Druids believed willow could help a person obtain guidance from the spirits in the Otherworld. Dowsers often use willow rods in their craft to locate hidden water.

GEMSTONE CHAKRA HEALING PRACTICE

According to Eastern healing teachings, our bodies receive cosmic light and vitality through spiritual energy centers known as chakras. *Chakra* is a Sanskrit word that means "wheel," and sensitive individuals who can see the chakras describe them as looking like spinning wheels of colored light. The seven major chakras run from the base of the spine to the top of the head, and correspond to the seven colors of the rainbow. Crystal workers often use gemstones of these seven colors to tune the body's aura and balance the flow of energy through the chakras. You can do this yourself—ask the elves, who have healing wisdom, to assist you.

You Will Need

- 1 red stone (such as red jasper, garnet, or red agate)
- 1 orange stone (such as tangerine quartz, topaz, or carnelian)
- 1 yellow stone (such as citrine, yellow zircon, or tiger's eye)
- 1 green stone (such as jade, malachite, or green agate)
- 1 light blue stone (such as turquoise, blue lace agate, or aquamarine)
- 1 dark blue stone (such as sapphire, lapis lazuli, or sodalite)
- 1 purple stone (such as amethyst, fluorite, or purple tourmaline) (all stones to be tumbled)
- Peaceful instrumental music (optional)
- A cloth or leather pouch
- Food for the elves

Directions

1. Wash the stones with mild soap and water before you begin working with them.

2. If you've chosen to listen to music, turn it on.

3. Lie on your back in a comfortable place where you won't be disturbed for a while.

4. Place the red stone near the base of your spine, what's known as the root chakra.

5. Place the orange stone on your abdomen, about a hand's width below your belly button, on the sacral chakra.

6. Place the yellow stone about halfway between your belly button and your heart. This is called the solar plexus chakra.

7. Place the green stone on your heart, the site of the heart chakra.

8. Place the light blue stone on the throat chakra, at the hollow between your collarbones at the base of your throat.

9. Place the dark blue stone on your third eye, between your eyebrows. This is called the brow chakra.

10. Place the purple stone at the top of your head, the crown chakra.

11. Close your eyes, relax, and let the gemstones gently bring your energy field into balance. You may feel them resonating on your

body, causing a slight tingling; perhaps you'll feel warmth or another sensation. Or, you might experience a quickening in the chakras as they open to allow more positive, healing energy in.

12. Remain like this for as long as you like, enjoying the healing benefits of the gemstones. Allow insights and information related to your overall well-being to enter your consciousness.

13. When you feel ready, open your eyes and remove the stones.

14. Store the stones in the pouch for future use. You can repeat this exercise whenever you like. It's especially helpful when you feel stressed out, devitalized, or just generally out of sorts.

15. Leave food for the elves to thank them for their assistance.

CHAKRA VISUALIZATION

This simple visualization focuses energy into the seven major chakras, to promote emotional and physical healing. Doing it as a daily meditation helps keep you balanced in mind and body, and in harmony with the universe. Even if you only spend 10 minutes a day, you'll notice benefits. Ask the elves to guide you and share their healing wisdom with you.

You Will Need
- Your book of shadows
- Food for the elves

Directions

1. Sit in a quiet, comfortable place where you won't be disturbed. Silence your phone, TV, and other distractions.

2. Close your eyes and take a few slow, deep breaths to relax.

3. Focus your attention on the root chakra at the base of your spine. Envision a bright red light glowing there.

4. Say aloud or in your mind:

> "I AM SAFE AND SECURE.
> I AM CONNECTED TO MOTHER EARTH AND NURTURED BY HER."

5. Shift your attention to your abdomen and the sacral chakra. Visualize a warm orange light glowing there.

6. Say aloud or in your mind:

"I AM CREATIVE.
I EXPRESS MYSELF JOYFULLY AND VIBRANTLY."

7. Focus your attention on your solar plexus chakra. Envision a lovely golden light glowing there.

8. Say aloud or in your mind:

"I AM COURAGEOUS AND CONFIDENT. I TRUST MYSELF AND KNOW I CAN HANDLE ANY CHALLENGE THAT COMES MY WAY."

9. Move your attention up to your heart chakra in the center of your chest. See a beautiful green light glowing there.

10. Say aloud or in your mind:

"I AM LOVED AND LOVABLE. I OPEN MY HEART TO GIVE AND RECEIVE LOVE."

11. Shift your attention to your throat chakra, between your collarbones at the base of your neck. Visualize sky-blue light glowing there.

12. Say aloud or in your mind:

"I AM HONEST. I SPEAK MY OWN TRUTH WITH CLARITY AND SINCERITY."

13. Focus your attention on your third eye chakra, between your eyebrows. Envision brilliant indigo light glowing there.

14. Say aloud or in your mind:

"I AM INTUITIVE. I BLEND INTUITION WITH INTELLECT AND AM GUIDED BY MY HIGHER SELF."

15. Move your attention up to the top of your head, the crown chakra. See rich purple light glowing there.

16. Say aloud or in your mind:

"I AM CONNECTED TO SOURCE, TO ALL THAT IS. I RECEIVE WISDOM, GUIDANCE, DIVINE LOVE, AND ALL I NEED FOR MY GREATEST GOOD."

17. At each step of this meditation, take time to let insights flow to you from spiritual sources. Allow your inner self to present thoughts, feelings, and impressions that will awaken healing knowledge within you.

18. Sit like this for as long as you like. When you feel ready, open your eyes and gradually return to your everyday awareness.

19. Write in your book of shadows whatever information you've received from the elves or your higher self during this meditation.

20. Thank the elves by leaving food for them in appreciation for their assistance.

BREW ELDERBERRY SYRUP TO CHASE A COLD

Elderberries are loaded with healthy benefits to relieve a cold, cough, or sore throat. They protect against viral and bacterial infection, support your immune system, have anti-inflammatory properties, and are high in antioxidants. On a spiritual level, the Druids believed the elder tree could cleanse unwanted energies from the psyche and soul, and enable people to excise their inner "demons." Elderberries also had the power to free people from the undue influence of others, thus allowing them to value themselves without relinquishing their sense of connection and responsibility to their clan. Ask the elves or pixies to guide you in making this elderberry syrup—and to share their healing secrets with you.

You Will Need

- A picture of an elder tree, downloaded from the Internet or from another source
- A pen or marker
- A medium-sized saucepan with lid
- 3 cups water
- 1 cup fresh elderberries or ⅔ cup dried berries
- 2 tablespoons fresh-grated ginger
- 1 teaspoon cinnamon
- ½ teaspoon ground cloves

- A wooden spoon
- A sieve or strainer
- A pitcher or large glass measuring cup with a spout
- ¾ cup honey (more if the brew isn't sweet enough for you)
- Lemon juice to taste
- Glass jars with lids

Directions

1. On the picture of the elder tree draw the Ogham symbol for it, *ruis*. Display it while you make this magick brew and contemplate the symbolism attached to this tree that the Druids considered sacred.

2. In the saucepan, add the water, elderberries, and spices.

3. Bring to a boil, stir, then cover the saucepan and simmer until the mixture is reduced by half (about 45 minutes).

4. Remove from the heat and let the brew cool.

5. Mash the berries with the spoon, then strain out the berries while pouring the liquid into the pitcher or measuring cup.

6. Stir in the honey until the syrup is smooth and well blended.

7. Add lemon juice to taste.

8. Pour the syrup into the glass jars and store them in the fridge.

9. Set out some of the syrup for the elves to thank them.

10. Take about a tablespoon of the syrup daily to strengthen your immune system or to ease the symptoms of a cold. As you ingest the syrup, look at the picture of the elder tree and contemplate its meaning. Sense its magick cleansing you of your "demons" so you can be at peace.

MORNING YOGA RITUAL FOR WELL-BEING

Greet each morning with a series of yoga postures called the *Surya Namaskar,* or Sun Salutation. This ritual loosens tight muscles, opens stiff joints, and frees stuck energy so it can flow smoothly through your body. It also calms your mind and helps you start the day on a positive note. Deep breathing is an important part of this ritual too. A central part of contemporary yoga practice since the early twentieth century, the Sun Salutation ritual may actually be two thousand years old. You can find instructions and illustrations of the poses online—in fact, you'll find several variations. Choose what works best for you. Start slow and build up to twelve repetitions. You may want to invite one of the Hindu fairies known as devas to join you—they understand the secrets to a long, healthy life.

You Will Need

- A gift of food for the fairies who help you

Directions

1. Stand facing east and say aloud:

> "I AM HEALED
> IN BODY AND MIND
> OF IMBALANCES
> OF ANY KIND."

2. Slowly go through the series of poses, matching your in- and out-breaths to the postures.

3. As you perform the movements, hold this incantation in your mind and feel body-mind healing taking place.

4. Turn to face the south and repeat the incantation aloud.

5. Slowly go through the series of poses again, matching your in- and out-breaths to the postures. You may sense the devas alongside you, shining and encouraging you like fairy personal trainers.

6. As you perform the movements, hold this incantation in your mind and feel body-mind healing taking place.

7. Turn to face the west and repeat the incantation aloud.

8. Slowly go through the series of poses again, matching your in- and out-breaths to the postures.

9. As you perform the movements, hold this incantation in your mind and feel body-mind healing taking place.

10. Turn to face the north and repeat the incantation aloud.

11. Slowly go through the series of poses again, matching your in- and out-breaths to the postures.

12. As you perform the movements, hold this incantation in your mind and feel body-mind healing taking place.

13. If you feel like doing another round, go for it. But don't strain yourself. This isn't a competition, and no one is judging your performance.

14. Leave a gift of food for the devas to thank them for their assistance. Devas like treats made with milk and honey or yogurt.

MAKE A HEALING HERBAL SALVE

Pure, organic essential oils offer gentle, natural healing for minor skin irritations, cuts, and scrapes. This easy-to-make salve combines three essential oils to provide relief, purification, and nourishment for your skin. You can purchase essential oils in health food stores or online. Ask the pixies to lend their energy and knowledge of botanicals to boost the benefits of your formulation.

You Will Need
- A glass jar with a lid
- 2 ounces of coconut oil
- 3 drops calendula essential oil
- 3 drops tea tree essential oil
- 3 drops lavender essential oil
- A spoon
- Food for the fairies

Directions
1. Wash the jar with mild soap and water.

2. Put the coconut oil in the jar.

3. Add the essential oils and stir.

4. As you stir, hold healing thoughts in your mind and project them into the mixture. You may sense the fairies adding their own magick to the concoction too.

5. Rub a little oil on your skin to soothe minor skin irritations or injuries.

6. Leave food for the pixies to thank them for their assistance.

7. Store the salve in a cool, dark place to prevent deterioration.

SYMPATHETIC MAGICK CANDLE SPELL

Sympathetic magick is a term used in spellcraft to describe the practice of using one item to represent or stand in for another. The two items bear some similarity to each other that signifies their connection. Ginseng root, for example, resembles the human body, a similarity that some healers believe contributes to ginseng's medicinal properties. The associations you make give the spell its direction and power. In this healing spell, you use a candle shaped like a human figure to symbolize you, and what you do to the candle energetically transfers to you. (You can also do this spell for someone else, but remember to get that person's permission first.) You can purchase these candles in metaphysical shops or online. If you're crafty, you may want to fashion your own from melted wax. I recommend using an unscented candle made of beeswax. Ask the elves to lend a hand—they're gifted healers.

You Will Need
- 1 candle shaped like a human being
- An athame, nail, nail file, ballpoint pen, or other sharp object
- Clippings of your hair and/or fingernails (optional)
- Essential oil—the type depends on the condition you intend to treat
- Healing products such as bandages, splints, salves, etc.—the type depends on the condition you intend to treat
- Matches or a lighter
- Food for the fae

Directions

1. On the candle, carve your name and your birthdate to identify it as your proxy.

2. If you like, affix the bits of your hair and/or nail clippings to the candle to further connect it with you. This isn't necessary, but it adds a little extra witchiness to the spell.

3. Apply the essential oil you've chosen to the wax figure's body part that requires attention. For example, if you have a chest cold you might rub some eucalyptus oil on the figure's chest. If you have an upset stomach, chamomile or peppermint oil would be a good choice.

4. Decide what other materials you'll need to treat the condition you are suffering from. For instance, if you have a broken leg and want to heal it quickly and successfully, you could fashion a splint and tie it around the candle figure's leg. If you have a cut on your arm you could put a bandage on the wax figure's arm.

5. Light the candle.

6. Visualize blue-green light surrounding the figure, soothing and healing the malady. Imagine yourself completely healed. In your mind's eye, see your body in perfect health—don't focus on the injury or ailment.

7. You may feel a sensation of tingling, warmth, relaxation, or something else in the area that's being treated. Perhaps you'll notice pain decreasing or tension easing.

8. Continue for as long as you like. When you feel it's time to stop, or your mind starts to wander, extinguish the candle. Leave whatever materials or remedies you've applied to the candle figure in place.

9. Set out food for the elf as a thank-you gift.

10. Repeat daily or as often as you choose until the condition is healed.

11. When you have recovered, remove the bandages or other materials from the figure and burn them. Wash the candle. Store it in a safe place for future use.

Chapter 10

WORKING WITH FAIRIES FOR PERSONAL AND PROFESSIONAL SUCCESS

We often equate success with a title, a position in a company or organization, or the amount of money we earn. But success is more than the rung you stand on in the corporate ladder. It's more than the number of games your athletic team won, the diplomas hanging on your walls, or the awards you've racked up over the years. As author Christopher Morley writes in *Where the Blue Begins*, "There is only one success—to be able to spend your life in your own way."

Many of us follow life paths that someone else set out for us, perhaps to fulfill their own dreams or agendas. Some of us get so caught up in society's expectations that we're no longer in touch with what's right for us, what fully engages our talents, skills, and potentials, what brings meaning and joy into our lives.

> "Two things are necessary for success in life; one is a sense of purpose and the other, a touch of madness. Hurl yourself at the thing you love and the entire Universe will come to your aid."
>
> JOHN HARRICHARAN, *Spirituality in Business*

ASKING FAIRIES FOR SUCCESS

Before you enact spells for personal and professional success, take some time to examine your ideas about what constitutes success. Are the ideas you hold the product of your own quest or someone else's desires? You may even want to make a list of the things that, as a child, you wanted to be "when you grew up." These may not have anything to do with your job, your status in society, or your financial situation—they may be related solely to what brings you happiness and a sense of fulfillment. After a bit of self-examination, you'll have a better sense of which fairies can assist you in your pursuits.

The spells in this chapter consider success in all areas of life, because really, all areas are connected. Instead of aiming only for fame and fortune, these spells help you access your own power and correct circumstances that may be sabotaging your happiness.

Which fairies are the best ones to help you succeed personally and/or professionally? Which can put you in touch with your goals and inspire you to achieve them? Which can teach you to sharpen your skills, improve your work habits, or ward off the competition?

- **LEPRECHAUNS:** These clever chaps can show you how to outwit competitors in the business world. They'll also assist people who work in financial fields, for they've got the inside track on matters pertaining to money. If you seek a better-paying job or want to get a raise, a leprechaun can offer tips to achieve your goal. Leprechauns have a fondness for music, so if you're looking to further a musical career or avocation, these are your go-to helpers.

- **ELVES:** These hardworking fairies are skilled artisans. If you're someone who works with your hands, in the trades or crafts, either as a vocation or avocation, an elf can offer invaluable guidance. Also known for their healing abilities, elves are often willing to aid people in the healthcare professions. If they take a liking to you or decide your efforts are worthwhile, they may assist you in any work-related endeavor.

- **BROWNIES:** Unassuming, diligent, and hardworking, brownies can give you the fortitude to tackle difficult or tedious tasks. They'll teach you the value of patience and perseverance in seeing a job through to the end. Brownies can also help you get organized, clear the clutter from your life, and become more productive.

- **SYLPHS:** These air spirits deal with mental areas—they're experts at handling situations that require a keen intellect, communication skills, or quick thinking. Ask for their assistance in understanding a challenging concept, giving a speech, composing a business proposal, or taking an exam. They might even slip you ideas for the Great American Novel.

THE ROAD TO SUCCESS

What does success mean to you? What goals do you seek to achieve during your sojourn on earth? Have you decided on a specific path in life, or are you still searching for the right one? This meditation lets you examine your direction and mentally experiment with possibilities. Along the way, you'll meet fairies who can offer advice, guidance, or perhaps companionship as you walk along the road to success.

You Will Need
- Your book of shadows

Directions

1. Sit in a comfortable place where you won't be disturbed. Silence your phone, TV, and other distractions.

2. Close your eyes and take several slow, deep breaths. Feel yourself relaxing, your mind growing quiet, your awareness opening.

3. Visualize yourself standing at the beginning of a road whose end you cannot see. Begin walking down the road. What kind of road is it? Dirt, rocky, or paved? Straight or winding? Level or hilly? Are you in the country, a forest, a city? Observe what lies ahead of you and what's on either side. Pay attention to details—they may be important.

4. Bring all your senses into the visualization. What's the weather like? What do you hear? Smell? How do you feel, physically and emotionally?

5. After a bit, you notice a fairy standing beside the road. What type of fairy is it? Approach it and ask if it has advice, guidance, or insights to share with you. Listen to the fairy's answer and contemplate what you've been told. Thank the fairy and continue on your way.

6. A little farther down the road you see a spirit animal standing beside the road. What type of creature is it? What significance does it have for you? Approach it and ask if it has advice, guidance, or insights to share with you. Listen to its reply, thank it, and continue on your way.

7. At some point, the road forks. Choose one fork and follow it. Is this path different than the previous one? In what way(s)? Why have you chosen this path?

8. Keep walking and encountering spirits along the road. Keep gathering information from them. They may offer tips that can help you reach your goal more quickly or suggest ways you can use your talents more effectively. They may point out beliefs or behaviors that are limiting you or interfering with your success.

9. As you meet and communicate with these spirits, notice how you feel in their presence. How do you react to what they share with you? Do you feel inspired or enlightened? Optimistic? Excited? Anxious? Resistant? Angry?

10. As you go along, you'll come to other forks and turns in the road. Perhaps you'll notice signs that point you in a particular direction. Maybe you'll cross a bridge or go through a gate. You might even encounter an obstacle that blocks your way, and you'll have to figure out how to get around it.

11. If you like, engage in different activities along the way. Which ones do you enjoy? Which are unpleasant or uncomfortable?

12. Continue for as long as you like. When you reach the end of the road, what do you find there? How do you feel about the journey and the destination at which you've arrived?

13. When you're ready, gradually return to your ordinary consciousness. Write in your book of shadows what you experienced and what insights you gained during the meditation.

SCRY TO SEE YOUR FUTURE

One of the most popular images people connect with witches, magick, and the psychic world is that of a seer gazing into a crystal ball to divine the future. The term "scry" means to look into a reflective surface in order to expand your vision, to see what can't be seen with your physical eyes. Remember the Wicked Queen who used a magick mirror in the fairy tale "Snow White and the Seven Dwarfs"? She was scrying. This spell lets you see what's likely to unfold for you in the near future, perhaps a few months from now. If you don't like what you see, start doing magick now to bring about the outcome you desire.

> "Look to the future, because that is where you'll spend the rest of your life."
>
> GEORGE BURNS, comedian

You Will Need

- A crystal ball (or other large quartz crystal); alternately, you can use a black mirror or a dark-colored bowl filled with water
- Small crystals for the fairies that help you
- Your book of shadows

Directions

1. Sit in a comfortable place where you won't be disturbed. Silence your phone, TV, and other distractions.

2. Close your eyes and envision yourself surrounded by a ball of pure white light, while you say aloud:

   "I AM PROTECTED BY DIVINE WHITE LIGHT, NOW AND ALWAYS."

3. Take several slow, deep breaths as you feel yourself relaxing, your mind growing quiet. Invite your fairy helpers to give you a sneak preview of what the future holds.

4. Set your crystal ball, magick mirror, or bowl of water on your altar, table, or another workplace.

5. Look into the shiny surface and let your gaze soften. Don't "try" to see anything in particular, just allow images to arise in the scrying device and in your mind's eye.

6. If you're using a crystal, you'll notice naturally occurring inclusions in the quartz, such as cloudy wisps, silver flakes, rainbows, openings that resemble tunnels, and maybe other smaller crystals growing inside. As you continue gazing into the crystal, these lights and shapes may begin to represent things to you.

7. You may see images or entire scenarios reflected in the scrying device. Or, you may get mental impressions, insights, or ideas about things to come, rather than actual pictures.

8. Continue scrying until you feel you've gotten what you sought or you start to lose your focus.

9. Thank your fairy helpers for their assistance and offer them small crystals to show your appreciation (not the crystal you've used for scrying, though). If you're working with a crystal, thank it as well.

10. In your book of shadows, write down what you witnessed. As your future unfolds, compare what you saw in advance with how things turned out.

MEDITATION TO REINVENT YOURSELF

Have you suffered a setback that has left you questioning your direction in life or even your own self-worth? Have you lost a job through no fault of your own and are now uncertain about your career path? Has the path you've followed for some time lost its luster, and you now seek meaning and fulfillment elsewhere? If so, this meditation can help you reconnect with your inner truth and what really matters to you in your heart of hearts. Ask the elves for guidance—elves are known for their ingenuity, craftsmanship, and healing abilities. They can help you make a new start or work through the challenging situation in which you now find yourself.

You Will Need
- Sandalwood incense in a holder
- Matches or a lighter
- Food for the elves

Directions

1. Set the incense on your altar or another place where it can burn safely and light it.

2. Silence your phone, TV, and other distractions. Sit in a comfortable place where you won't be disturbed for a while.

3. Close your eyes and take a few slow, deep breaths to calm your mind.

4. Imagine you are standing in the elves' workshop. Take a few moments to look around the workshop and get comfortable with your surroundings.

5. You see three elves there. Ask them to help you reinvent yourself and watch as they nod their heads in assent.

6. Notice you are wearing old, worn-out clothes and shoes. One of the elves tells you to remove your clothes—they are going to make new ones for you. In your mind's eye, see yourself following their instructions.

7. One elf takes your measurements and draws a pattern on a piece of paper. Another selects bolts of fabric from a shelf. A third chooses leather for a pair of shoes.

8. While you watch, the elves busy themselves with cutting, stitching, gluing, performing all the tasks involved in creating a new outfit for you to wear. Notice how joyfully they go about their job, whistling while they work. Just being in their presence makes you feel more hopeful and confident about your future.

9. When they've finished, one of the elves tells you to put on the new outfit they've made for you. Another hands you the new shoes to wear.

10. Visualize yourself putting on the new clothing. As you button, zip, and tie, feel a sense of optimism and excitement coming over you. Look in a mirror and see yourself glowing with happiness. Notice how perfectly everything fits, how comfortable you are wearing these wondrous garments.

11. One of the elves burns your old clothes, and you feel a delicious sense of freedom as you watch them go up in smoke.

12. When you feel ready, thank the elves and leave their workshop. Return to your ordinary awareness and open your eyes.

13. Leave food outside for the elves as a thank-you gift.

> "Success is measured not so much by the position that one has reached in life as by the obstacles which he has overcome while trying to succeed."
>
> BOOKER T. WASHINGTON, educator

GEMSTONE TALISMAN FOR SUCCESS

This talisman invites success to come your way, in whatever area you desire. Do you seek a plum career position? Do you hope to win an athletic competition? Do you long for recognition in your creative endeavors? Whatever you desire is within the realm of possibility— so long as you believe in yourself and the likelihood of your success. This talisman is designed to attract success in general; however, you can fine-tune it to serve your immediate purposes by adding gems that have specific connections to your intention. Invite the elves and/ or pixies to join you in preparing the talisman.

You Will Need
- 1 piece of tumbled golden topaz
- 1 piece of tumbled hematite
- 1 piece of tumbled tiger's eye
- 1 piece of tumbled turquoise
- 1 piece of tumbled star sapphire
- 1 piece of tumbled onyx

- 1 piece of tumbled jade
- 1 piece of tumbled aventurine
- 1 gold-colored drawstring pouch
- Sandalwood incense in a holder
- Matches or a lighter
- Food for the fairies

Directions

1. One by one, slip the eight gemstones into the pouch. Eight is the number of success in the material world.

2. Imagine you are standing at the foot of a staircase with eight steps. Each time you put a stone into the pouch, visualize yourself mounting a step.

3. Continue adding gemstones to the pouch while you climb the stairs. Each stone and each step bring you closer to your goal.

4. When you reach the top, see yourself happily receiving the success and accolades you deserve. Enjoy the feeling of accomplishment, of arriving where you want to be in life at this time.

5. Set the incense on your altar, table, or another surface and light it.

6. Hold the pouch that contains the gemstones in the incense smoke to charge it.

7. Leave food for the fairies to thank them for their assistance.

8. Carry the pouch with you until you achieve the goal you seek.

Fairy Crystals

Some quartz crystals are thought to have special links to fairies. Fairy wands, for example, look like tiny scepters or towers in miniature castles. Fairy clusters contain numerous long, thin, delicate points joined at the crystal's base. Fairy frost crystals have patterns inside them that resemble frost on a windowpane. People who work with fairy crystals say these stones have been touched by fairies, and, as a result, they emit joyful, positive vibrations. Some crystal enthusiasts believe meditating with fairy crystals can put you in touch with the spirit realm.

CONCOCT A CONFIDENCE POTION

It's natural to feel a bit anxious when you're facing a challenge. You have a secret weapon to combat anxiety, however. Magick can help calm your nerves and boost your self-confidence. Ask the undines to assist you in concocting this magick potion. They never question their ability to handle problems, nor do they worry about how situations will turn out.

You Will Need

- A small glass bottle with a lid, with no pictures, words, or other markings on it
- 3 ounces of spring water
- Bergamot essential oil
- The Sun card from a tarot deck

Directions

1. Wash the bottle with mild soap and water, and let it dry in the sun.

2. Pour the water into the bottle.

3. Add several drops of essential oil, whatever strength smells good to you.

4. Put the lid on the bottle and shake it three times to charge it.

5. Lay The Sun card faceup on a windowsill.

6. Set the bottle on the card. If possible, do this the night before you must face the challenge, and leave the card and bottle in place overnight. If you can position it in a spot where the moon will shine on it, so much the better. In the morning, replace the tarot card in its deck.

7. Before you face the challenge, shake the bottle, uncap it, and smell the pleasing aroma. Dab some of the magick potion on your solar plexus chakra.

8. Close your eyes and apply gentle pressure to your solar plexus for about a minute, while you envision yourself completely surrounded by glowing golden light.

9. Feel your worries dissipating, your confidence growing. Believe that you will succeed in whatever you do, and sense the undines nearby, offering encouragement.

10. Empty the rest of the potion into a body of water as a gift for the undines.

RITUAL TO OPEN NEW DOORS

This ritual uses the power of symbolism and suggestion to bring new opportunities your way. If an area of your life seems stuck, or you feel it's time to shift your direction, perform this ritual with the fairies. If you seek to stimulate changes in your career, ask the elves to join you. If you want to open possibilities in your love life, the undines can help. Partner with the sylphs to embark on a new course of study or another intellectual path.

You Will Need

- A gift for the fairies (the type of gift depends on which fairies help you)

Directions

1. Go through the interior of your home, room by room, and open all the doors.

2. Next, open the doors to closets and cabinets.

3. If weather and other conditions permit, open the exterior doors and windows.

4. Mentally or verbally invite new opportunities to come to you.

5. As you open the doors, sense the "stuck" energy in your home loosening and beginning to shift. Even if you aren't able to open the exterior doors and windows, the air may feel fresher,

brighter, lighter. Let your mind release old beliefs, negativity, and self-limiting ideas that have created obstructions.

6. When you've finished, close the doors and windows.

7. Leave the gift you've chosen for the fae who helped you.

Feng Shui Magick

The ancient Chinese art of placement known as feng shui considers your home to be a reflection of you. It's actually a type of magick. Like all magick, feng shui uses intention, symbolism, and imagination to create successful outcomes. According to this school of thought, closets jam-packed with stuff you don't use cause blockages and limitations. To make room for new opportunities, you need to get rid of old things. Clean out that clutter and see how quickly changes start to happen.

CANDLE SPELL TO ATTRACT NEW BUSINESS

Witches use candles in all sorts of spells—candles can augment virtually any ritual, mundane or magickal. Candles symbolize hope, brighter times, inspiration, and clarity. They also signify Spirit. This spell taps the positive symbolism associated with candles to attract new clients, customers, investors, or opportunities. Ask the fire spirits and/or the sylphs—whom some people describe as looking like tiny flames or twinkling lights—to join you.

You Will Need
- Cedar essential oil
- 1 white candle in a candleholder
- 7 candles, 1 of each color of the rainbow, in candleholders
- Matches or a lighter
- A piece of green, gold, or silver cloth
- 1 piece of tumbled carnelian

Directions

1. Use the essential oil to dress all eight candles. Eight is the number of business and financial success in the material world. Cedar is an oil witches connect with abundance.

2. Set the white candle in the middle of your altar or another spot where it can burn safely and remain in place for three days. This candle represents you/your business.

3. Arrange the other candles in a circle around the white candle. The rainbow-colored candles should be positioned about a foot away from the white candle. These candles represent whom/what you intend to attract.

4. Light the candles and let them burn for at least 10 minutes, while you visualize your objective. Then snuff out the candles.

5. On the second day, move the multicolored candles closer to the white candle.

6. Light the candles and let them burn for at least 10 minutes, while you visualize your objective. Then snuff out the candles.

7. On the third day, move the multicolored candles closer together, until they are touching either the white candle or each other.

8. Light the candles and let them burn for at least 10 minutes, while you visualize your objective. Then snuff out the candles.

9. Remove what's left of the candles from their holders and wrap them in the piece of cloth. Store them in a safe spot at your workplace.

10. Leave the carnelian for the fairies as a thank-you gift.

> "Thousands of candles can be lit from a single candle, and the life of the candle will not be shortened. Happiness never decreases by being shared."
>
> **THE BUDDHA**, spiritual leader

USE A PENDULUM TO MAKE A CAREER DECISION

A pendulum usually consists of a small weight, such as a crystal, hanging from a short chain or cord. You hold the chain, letting the pendulum dangle at the end of it, while you ask a simple question.

The pendulum's movement—back and forth, side to side, around and around—has meaning and provides answers to your question. The pendulum swings of its own accord. When you consult a pendulum for the purpose of divination, you're searching for answers hidden deep within yourself. Ask the air spirits known as sylphs to guide you and help you gain the insight you seek.

You Will Need

- Sandalwood incense in a holder
- Matches or a lighter
- A feather
- A pendulum

Directions

1. Place the incense on your altar or table and light it to honor the sylphs. They also like feathers, so lay one there for them as a gift.

2. Silence your phone, TV, and other distractions. Sit in a comfortable place, at a table, for example, where you can rest your elbow on a steady surface.

3. Close your eyes and take a few deep breaths to calm and center your mind. Contemplate the question you want answered or the condition about which you seek advice.

4. When you feel ready, open your eyes. Rest your elbow on the table for support and hold the pendulum so that its bob is about 6 inches above the tabletop. Don't grip it; hold it loosely so it can swing easily.

5. Ask your question or state your request aloud, in simple, unambiguous terms. For example, you might ask if you should accept a particular job offer or whether a job-related matter will turn out in your favor. Or, you might ask if following a certain career path is right for you.

6. Soon, the pendulum should start to move—don't try to influence its movement, though.

7. If the pendulum swings from side to side, the answer is no.

8. If the pendulum swings back and forth, forward and backward, the answer is yes.

9. If the pendulum circles in a clockwise direction, the situation is favorable.

10. If the pendulum circles in a counterclockwise direction, the situation is unfavorable.

11. If the pendulum moves along a diagonal line, an answer isn't possible at this time.

12. If the pendulum remains motionless for more than a minute or so, try asking the question in a different way. A question like "What career is right for me?" is impossible to answer, but "Is a career in veterinary medicine right for me?" should produce a result.

13. Some witches like to use a divining board that has words on it such as yes, no, maybe, now, later, etc. Hold the pendulum above the board and allow the bob to swing toward those words, if they apply to the situation. After you've become familiar with pendulum divination, you can design your own methods for working with your pendulum.

WITCH'S STEW FOR SUCCESS

Artists often depict the Irish goddess Brigid stirring a bubbling cauldron in which she blends the physical and spiritual ingredients that nurture us. Cauldrons symbolize the womb and represent fertility. As the goddess of inspiration, Brigid encourages everyone, regardless of gender, to stir the cauldron of creativity that exists within each of us. Cauldrons also serve a practical purpose: for cooking ritual meals. If weather permits, you may be able to make this magick stew over an outdoor fire. Otherwise your kitchen range or a wood-burning stove, if you have one, will suffice. While you're cooking, keep your intention in mind and project it mentally into the stew you're preparing. Invite household fairies, such as the brownies or kobolds, to participate in the meal's preparation.

You Will Need

- 1 tablespoon olive oil (more if needed)
- A cauldron (or cooking pot)
- 2 pounds uncooked beef, cut into bite-sized chunks
- ¼ cup flour
- 1 medium garlic clove, chopped
- 1 medium yellow onion, chopped
- 6 baby bella mushrooms, chopped
- 1 beef bouillon cube, dissolved in water
- 1 (8-ounce) can tomato sauce
- 12 whole black peppercorns
- 6 whole cloves
- 1 bay leaf
- 1 teaspoon dried basil or 2 fresh basil leaves, chopped
- 4 ounces dry red wine
- 3 medium redskin potatoes, chopped
- 6 medium carrots, chopped
- A handful (or more) green beans, chopped

Directions

1. Pour the oil into the heated cauldron or pot.

2. Add the beef chunks and stir in a clockwise direction (to encourage increase) until browned.

3. Sprinkle flour over the beef and stir until all beef chunks are covered in flour.

4. Add garlic, onion, and mushrooms and stir in a clockwise direction until onion pieces are translucent but not browned.

5. Add bouillon, tomato sauce, peppercorns, cloves, bay leaf, basil, and wine. Stir in a clockwise direction.

6. Cover the cauldron and simmer over low heat for about 2 hours or until the beef is tender enough to pierce easily with a fork.

7. Add potatoes, carrots, and green beans, cover again, and cook for another 45 minutes or so.

8. On a cold fall or winter night, this hearty witch's stew is a welcome dish to share with friends and loved ones. Remember to set a bowl out for the fairies to thank them for using their magick powers to foster your success.

BURN OGHAM LETTERS TO BRING SUCCESS

In Chapter 4 we talked about the Ogham alphabet that's based on the wisdom and powers of trees. To the ancient Druids, trees were considered sentient, sacred, magickal beings that could teach us a great deal. In this spell, you use the symbolism inherent in the Ogham letters to attract the success you desire. Instead of burning the actual wood from the trees, you burn their glyphs. The nature spirits who care for trees can help you enact this ritual.

You Will Need
- Slips of paper
- A pen, pencil, marker, or other writing utensil
- A cauldron, barbecue grill, hibachi, or fireplace
- Matches or a lighter
- Your book of shadows
- Food for the nature spirits

Directions
1. Select one (or more) Ogham letter that describes your goal. For example, if you seek a new job, birch/*beth* is a good rune to choose because it represents beginnings and new opportunities. You can find more information about Ogham and Celtic tree magick in *The Modern Guide to Witchcraft* and in Steve Blamires's book *Celtic Tree Mysteries*, or online.

2. On one slip of paper, write your primary objective. Additionally, draw the Ogham letter that most closely aligns with your intention(s). If you feel a need for courage and determination in pursuing your goals, draw the glyph for alder/*fearn* on the paper. If you seek knowledge and guidance from otherworldly sources that

can show you how to advance in your career, sketch the rune for hazel/*coll.*

3. On other slips of paper draw the runes that relate to what you desire—as many as you choose.

4. When you've finished, gather the slips of paper that contain your wishes. Lay them in your cauldron. You can also use a fireplace, barbecue grill, fire pit, hibachi, or other place where you can burn a small fire safely.

5. Light the fire and, as you stare into the flames, imagine the sacred trees symbolized on the slips of paper you're burning. Contemplate their meanings and the teachings they offer you. Allow their insights to enter your awareness. Record them in your book of shadows after you've completed this spell.

6. Let the fire die down. Let the ashes cool.

7. Scatter the ashes from the fire at the base of an oak tree.

8. Leave food for the fairies who have assisted you to thank them.

AMULET TO PROTECT YOUR JOB

Do you fear your job is in danger, perhaps due to cutbacks or competition? This amulet protects your current position. However, before you perform the spell, make certain you really want to stay in this job—it's possible that if you lost it something better might come to you. Ask the elves to assist you—these skillful and hardworking fairies understand the importance of gainful employment, not only for financial security but also for self-esteem and the experiences of working with other people.

You Will Need
- A symbol or image that represents your job—a photo of you performing your job, a logo, etc. (you can download images from the Internet)
- A black pouch, preferably made of silk
- A small pentagram

- Dried basil
- Dried rosemary
- Dried fennel
- An ash leaf
- A small pine cone or pine needles
- An 8-inch-long piece of gold-colored cord or ribbon
- Pine incense in a holder
- Matches or a lighter
- Food for the elves

Directions

1. Put the image or symbol in the pouch.

2. Slip the pentagram into the pouch.

3. Add the herbs, the ash leaf, and the pine cone or needles.

4. Close the pouch with the cord or ribbon, making eight knots. Each time you tie a knot say aloud:

> "I AM SAFE AND HAPPY IN MY JOB AT ALL TIMES AND IN ALL SITUATIONS, FOR AS LONG AS I CHOOSE."
> (Or, compose your own affirmation.)

5. Light the incense and hold the pouch in the smoke to charge it.

6. Put the amulet in your desk drawer or other spot in your workplace to safeguard your job.

7. Leave food for the elves to thank them for helping you.

CREATE WITCH BOTTLES FOR YOUR FRIENDS

In Chapter 1 you read about the nineteenth-century Irish herbalist "Biddy" Early, who owned a mysterious magick bottle that supposedly contained the fairies' healing secrets. Witch or spell bottles hold items with similar energies, brought together for a specific intention. You can include crystals, herbs, or whatever symbolizes your objective. Focus on only one objective per bottle—all items should resonate with the energy of that objective. For example, if you're making a witch bottle for someone who wants to win an important ball game, include items that will help your friend accomplish that goal, such as oak for strength, carnelian for vitality and enthusiasm, and so on. If another friend hopes to get a new job, choose ingredients to further that end. Refer to the Appendix at the back of the book for lists of correspondences. Ask the fairies to add their magick to the bottles.

You Will Need

- 1 small, clear glass bottle with a lid for each friend
- 1 orange candle in a candleholder
- Cinnamon essential oil
- Matches or a lighter
- A small piece of paper
- A ballpoint pen
- Crystals, gemstones, shells, flower petals, herbs, feathers, milagros—whatever objects you choose to represent your intention
- Ribbons in colors that relate to your intention
- Food for the fairies

Directions

1. Wash the bottles with mild soap and water, and set them in the sun to dry.

2. Dress the orange candle with the essential oil and light it. Orange is a color witches associate with success. Let the candle burn while you do the rest of this spell.

3. On the piece paper, write your intention for one friend. You may do this in the form of an affirmation, for example, "Paul's team wins the championship game." Or, you can design a sigil that represents the result you seek (see Chapter 7 for instructions).

4. Roll the paper like a scroll and slip it into the bottle. Sense the fairies whispering their magick into the bottle too.

5. Add the various ingredients you've chosen to the bottle, and then close it.

6. Drip candle wax on the lid to seal it. While the wax is still soft, use the pen to write something, such as your friend's initials, in the wax to personalize the witch bottle.

7. Tie the ribbons around the neck of the bottle. As you tie them, visualize your friend achieving the goal he or she desires.

8. Repeat this procedure for each friend to whom you'll give a witch bottle.

9. Leave food outside for the fairies to thank them for their assistance.

ONGOING RITUAL FOR CONTINUED SUCCESS

Throughout our lives we'll experience numerous successes, large and small, in many areas both personal and professional. We'll also suffer some "failures," which may actually be bridges to further success. Over time, your successes and failures—as well as your perceptions of them—will change. This ritual keeps your mind focused on your objectives day by day and helps you value the process as well as the end result. Writing down your intentions moves them one step closer to manifestation by bringing your thoughts out of the abstract realm and into the field of physical reality. You may choose to engage fairies in the process—which fairies you interact with will depend on your intentions. Unpretentious brownies, who exhibit persistence in their dedication to daily practices and tasks, may help you understand the importance of small, mundane successes as well as glorious ones.

You Will Need
- 1 candle of a color you like or 1 that relates to your intention, in a candleholder
- Matches or a lighter
- Your book of shadows
- A pen, pencil, or marker
- Food for the fairies

Directions

1. Set aside some time each day to focus on a desired objective in your personal or professional life, or both. Ideally, you'll want to do this early in the day, before mundane distractions interfere, and at the same time every day. Your subconscious likes routines, and once you train it, it will shift into gear as the appointed time approaches.

2. Light a candle to signify that you are "turning on the light" and welcoming the new day, inviting inspiration, clarity, and wisdom to come to you.

3. In your book of shadows, write one hope, objective, or plan for the day.

4. Next, find an inspiring quote about success on the Internet, in a book, or elsewhere and jot it down in your book of shadows.

5. Write a thought about your aspirations, your values, or what success means to you. You might add a comment about why you think this way.

6. Describe where you choose to direct your energy today. Is a particular challenge facing you? Do you have an opportunity to embrace? What step will help you achieve your goal or fulfill your purpose today?

7. Mention something you sought to achieve earlier in your life that you have now accomplished. Allow yourself to feel satisfaction at having successfully finished what you set out to do. Little things matter just as much as big ones.

8. If you've had a dream that seems relevant, that offers direction, that answers a problem, or another form of advice, note it in your book of shadows.

9. When you've finished, snuff out the candle.

10. At the end of the day, light the candle again.

11. Write in your book about how your intentions materialized today. What progress did you make? What did you learn? What adjustments did you make, if any? How were you guided/helped?

Acknowledge your accomplishments, however small. Over time, you may find it interesting to see how your ideas have changed, how your journey has evolved, and how much you've achieved.

12. Thank any fairy helpers who may have assisted you by leaving food outside for them.

> "The past is history, the future is a mystery, and this moment is a gift. That is why this moment is called 'the present.'"
>
> **DEEPAK CHOPRA,** *The Seven Spiritual Laws of Success*

Chapter 11

WORKING WITH FAIRIES FOR PERSONAL AND SPIRITUAL GROWTH

Our lives are never static. We're constantly engaged in the process of growth and self-improvement, whether or not we're aware of it. Some spiritual teachers say that's our main purpose for taking on a human form and residence on Planet Earth. Our time here is equivalent to enrollment in a school where we gain wisdom, polish off the rough edges of our beings, and gather up material our souls can apply in future incarnations.

Most likely, your possibilities are endless, just as the universe in which we exist is endless. We need only open ourselves to those possibilities, instead of narrowing our options based on what other people think we should do to improve ourselves. Instead of forcing ourselves into roles that society, our families and loved ones, our religious institutions, or other "authorities" deem appropriate, we may need to devote some time to deciding what avenues we want to explore, what mountains we want to climb, in order to become the glorious beings we truly are.

INVITING THE FAE INTO YOUR LIFE

In this chapter you'll find spells, rituals, and other practices to help you expand into areas you may not have been aware of before. They can also aid you in the development of your innate talents and powers. Several of these practices involve journeying to realms of experience beyond the physical plane with which you're familiar, something shamans and witches around the world have engaged in for millennia. Because fairies do this sort of thing all the time and are masters at walking between the worlds, you may choose to solicit their assistance as your guides. You can even visit fairyland. The lessons you learn from the fae will awaken your consciousness and catapult you into new areas of knowledge, awareness, and power.

"Each day comes bearing its own gifts. Untie the ribbons."

RUTH ANN SCHABACKER, author

Which fairies are the best ones to aid you in your personal growth and self-improvement? Which will support and encourage your quest for meaning, understanding, and joy? How can your explorations of the fairy worlds benefit you in the earth realm, now and in future incarnations?

- **SYLPHS:** These air spirits can assist with intellectual development, communication, and mental tasks.

- **SALAMANDERS:** If you seek inspiration, courage, or zest for life, these fire spirits can lend their energy to spells and other magickal practices.

- **LEPRECHAUNS:** These wily characters can teach you cunning and cleverness.

- **BEAN SIDHES:** In times of transition, loss, or grief, the *bean sidhe* can help you see the big picture and connect you with the ongoing cycle of life, death, and rebirth. A *bean sidhe* can also teach you how to communicate with loved ones on the Other Side.

- **GROGOCHES:** Unpretentious and hardworking grogoches can show you the benefits of modesty, persistence, and patience.

- **FAIRY ANIMALS:** Animal spirits can lend you their innate characteristics as needed, such as speed, strength, stealth, agility, and so on.

WITCH'S LADDER

A witch's ladder is a construction of yarn, ribbons, string, and/or other material knotted or braided together to form a length of entwined fabric for spiritual and/or magickal purposes. Some sources say it serves as a counting device, similar to a rosary, that allows the user to keep track of prayers by fingering the knots. Witches familiar with knot magick use the ladder to tie intentions into the plait. This spell is designed to boost your intellectual ability, memory, and concentration. Use it when you're studying for an exam, preparing a business proposal, or writing a novel. Invite one or more sylphs to join you in creating this talisman.

You Will Need

- 8 pieces of yellow or blue yarn, ribbon, or string, each at least 3 feet long
- Clear quartz beads, as many as you choose
- Feathers found in the wild (not plucked from a living bird)
- Sandalwood incense in an incense holder
- Matches or a lighter

Directions

1. Tie the three pieces of yarn, ribbon, or string together at one end. Three is the number of manifestation in the physical world. With this spell, you bring your intention into three-dimensional existence.

2. Fit the beads onto the fabric. Sense the sylphs guiding your fingers, lending their energy to your spell.

3. Begin knotting the three piece of fabric together. With each knot you tie, state your intention aloud.

4. Tie the feathers into the knots. Feathers symbolize the air element, which magick practitioners associate with mental activity and communication.

5. Keep your attention focused on your objective until you've finished tying nine knots. Nine, the last single digit and the equivalent of three times three, is the number of completion. As you tie the last knot, say: "So MOTE IT BE" to seal the spell.

6. Set the incense in its holder on your altar (or another surface) and light it. This is your thank-you gift to the sylphs.

7. Display the ladder on your altar or another place where you'll see it often. You may choose to carry it with you when you take a test, give a speech, make a presentation, etc.

8. When the ladder has served its purpose, burn or bury it.

SEE FAIRYLAND THROUGH A HAG STONE

A hag stone—alternately called a fairy stone, witch stone, holey stone, or Odin stone—is one that has a naturally occurring hole in it. The hole is caused by water rubbing away at the stone over a long time, so the best places to look for them are in a stream, river, or by the ocean. Legends say that by looking through the hole you can expand your vision to view places you couldn't ordinarily see with your physical eyes.

What Are Hags?

These fairies usually look like old women, although they can transform themselves into beautiful young women if they choose. The term is often used interchangeably for spirits as well as for female human elders with magickal powers. In folklore, they're described as having healing power and "the Sight." Perhaps the most familiar hags in the English-speaking world are the three witches in Shakespeare's *Macbeth*, who chant "toil and trouble" while stirring their strange brew.

You Will Need

- 1 or more hag stones
- Your book of shadows

Directions

1. Ideally, you'll want to find hag stones in nature. However, if that's not feasible, you can purchase them online or in shops that sell minerals, crystals, etc.

2. Cleanse and clear the stone before using it. You can do this easily by washing it with mild soap and water, then leaving it in the sunlight to dry. Envision the stone surrounded and infused by pure white light to remove any unwanted energies. You've now transformed an ordinary stone into a tool for working magick.

3. Set your intention to see fairyland, then look through the hole in the stone. Allow your gaze to soften. Try not to hold on to expectations—just let your mind grow quiet and calm. Whatever you see is what you are supposed to see, what the fairies are willing to let you see at this time.

4. You can also use a hag stone to see into the future or into other realms of existence. Or, peek through the hole to view something that's hidden from your everyday sight, that's too distant to observe with your physical eyes, or perhaps one that's otherwise a secret.

5. As you continue practicing this technique, you'll notice your senses growing keener, your vision sharper, your awareness greater. Record what you witness in your book of shadows.

GAIN WISDOM FROM A TREE

Each tree has wisdom to impart—old trees especially, for they've survived hundreds of years on earth and acquired a great deal of experience. The rings that develop in tree trunks not only tell of weather conditions, insect infestation, and other physical events; they also contain and chronicle the emotional experiences the tree has undergone over its long life.

How Texas Trees Got Their Names

In Texas, where I live, trees were sometimes named for the experiences that took place in their presence: weddings, hangings, battles, treaties negotiated. The Tragedy Tree in Bandera got its name due to a triple hanging during the Civil War. The thousand-year-old Bishop's Tree in Goose Island State Park was once the site of the Karankawa Indians' ceremonies. In her novel *The Which Way Tree*, author Elizabeth Crook recounts the story of making a life decision. Those episodes not only remain as part of history; they also infiltrate the psychic makeup of the trees themselves.

You Will Need

- A small vial of red wine
- Your book of shadows

Directions

1. Set aside time each week to spend with a tree that's special to you. Or, go into the woods and interact with many trees there.

2. Sit beneath a tree in your yard, in a forest, or in a public park. If you feel up to it, climb the tree and sit among its branches. Lean your back against its trunk. Run your hands along its bark. Stroke its leaves. Inhale its scent. Listen to its leaves rustle as the wind blows through them.

3. Try to sense the presence of a forest fairy or dryad in residence in the tree. Perhaps you'll notice a "face" in the tree's bark smiling at you.

4. Hug the tree. Sing to it. Dance around it. Thank it for the shelter and habitat it provides to birds and animals, for its role in cleansing our air, for the shade it offers on hot summer days, for the wood its relatives have given us to build our homes and cook our meals.

5. Ask the tree to share its secrets with you. Be quiet and listen carefully. Trees communicate telepathically, and their "speech" is slow compared to ours.

6. At the end of your meeting with the trees, pour the wine on the ground nearby as a gift to the forest fairies who inhabit and care for the trees.

7. You may choose to continue developing a relationship with one special tree, or to engage in conversations with a number of trees. Each tree has its own characteristics, powers, and knowledge.

8. In your book of shadows, record your conversations with the tree(s). What did you experience? What insights did you gain? What creatures, physical or nonphysical, did you observe?

The Celtic Tree Calendar

Researchers Maya Magee Sutton and Nicholas R. Mann, authors of *Druid Magic*, describe the connections between trees and specific times of the year. If you choose to do magick with trees, you may achieve better results or gain more meaningful insights if you align yourself with the trees whose energies harmonize with the periods listed here.

Samhain through Yule: elder, blackthorn, reed
Yule through Imbolc: reed, ivy, bramble
Imbolc through Ostara: apple, hazel, holly
Ostara through Beltane: holly, oak, hawthorn
Beltane through Midsummer: willow, alder, ash
Midsummer through Lughnasadh: rowan, birch
Lughnasadh through Mabon: yew, poplar, heather
Mabon through Samhain: heather, gorse, fir

SHAMANIC JOURNEYING WITH A TREE

Witches who work with the fae often take shamanic journeys to other realms of experience beyond what we're familiar with in our everyday earthly lives. A shaman is someone who "walks between the worlds" and may interact with the entities that occupy the worlds beyond. You travel in spirit, not physically. In Chapter 4 we talked about the Otherworld and the Underworld, but many levels of reality exist, and you can visit them if you choose. You can elect to go to a certain place, or you may prefer to just allow your inner self to take you wherever you can benefit most at this time. If you've established a relationship with a particular fairy who can serve as your guide and co-walker, ask that fairy to join you.

You Will Need

- A recording of rhythmic drumming
- A pentagram or protection amulet, such as the one described in Chapter 8
- Your book of shadows
- A gift for the fairy (if a fairy accompanies you)

Directions

1. Silence all distractions. Turn off your phone, TV, etc. Close pets away where they won't bother you. If you live with other people, instruct them not to disturb you. This journey can take a half hour or longer.

2. Turn on the recording of the drumming. The drumming should not have a catchy beat, nor should it be accompanied by a tune or words.

3. Hold/wear the pentagram or protection amulet.

4. Sit in a comfortable place. Close your eyes and envision yourself surrounded by a ball of pure white light, while you say aloud:

   "I AM PROTECTED BY DIVINE WHITE LIGHT, NOW AND ALWAYS."

5. Take several slow, deep breaths as you feel yourself relaxing, your mind growing quiet.

6. Listen to the drumming and let it slowly shift you out of your ordinary consciousness into a light trance state. You are aware of your body but feel emotionally detached from it.

7. In your mind's eye, see a huge tree with branches that stretch high into the sky, beyond the clouds. Hundreds of branches reach out in all directions. The tree is so tall you can't see its top. The trunk is so thick that twenty people holding hands couldn't reach around it. Its gnarled roots delve deep into the ground, but parts of them wind along the surface of the earth like enormous serpents.

8. Approach the tree, and as you get closer, notice an opening at the base of the trunk. The opening is large enough for you to enter.

9. Crawl through the opening, into the tree's trunk, and stand up. Inside it's too dark to see, but you sense a hollow space, like a vertical tunnel running up through the center of the tree's trunk.

10. Feel yourself gently being drawn up through the vertical tunnel, as if you were riding in a slow-moving elevator. You may sense a special fairy guide accompanying you. Or, you may be aware of the presence of nature spirits that the ancient Greeks called dryads who reside in and enliven the tree.

11. As you rise through the tree's trunk, you realize you can feel what the tree feels. You know what the tree knows. This wise old tree is passing on its wisdom to you, the knowledge it has gained during its long, long life.

12. When you finally reach the tree's canopy, high above the clouds, choose a branch and envision yourself moving along that branch. At the end, look around. Where are you?

13. Take time to observe the world that unfolds before you. What is it composed of? How does it feel to you? Do you hear sounds? Smell aromas? See colors? Who or what inhabits this world? If you witness sentient beings there, what are they like? Can you interact with them? How do you relate? Can you communicate? What information do they share with you?

14. If you like, you can step off the branch and explore this world further. Or, you can remain on the branch, observing.

15. Spend as long as you like in this place. Pay close attention and try to commit what you experience to memory, so you can bring it back with you into your ordinary world.

16. When you feel ready, move back along the tree branch and into the "elevator shaft" in the trunk. Sense yourself gently descending.

17. When you reach the ground, thank the tree for granting you passage to another realm of existence. Thank it for the wisdom it has shared with you.

18. Gradually return to your ordinary, everyday awareness. Take whatever time you need to resettle into your physical body.

19. Record what you experienced in your book of shadows.

20. If a fairy accompanied you on your shamanic journey, leave it a thank-you gift of food or something else that you deem appropriate.

> "To Druids, then, the many trees represent everything in existence: each tree has attributes that correspond to related human, nature-based, and spirit essences. The symbology provided by the entire assembly of the trees puts order into all the realms in the universe."
>
> MAYA MAGEE SUTTON and NICHOLAS R. MANN, *Druid Magic*

TRANSFORM OBSTACLES INTO OPPORTUNITIES

Witches use fire as a tool for transformation, both to destroy and to create. Often these two seemingly opposite actions occur in concert—the old must be eliminated before the new can be born. Think of the mythical phoenix that rises from the ashes. We link the fire element with creativity, action, and the will to make things happen. You can also employ fire energy to banish fear, or in purification spells and rituals. In this fire ritual, you release old, self-limiting beliefs and inspire new possibilities. Invite the fire spirits known as salamanders to join you.

> "I will release this list of my desires and surrender it to the womb of creation, trusting that when things don't seem to go my way, there is a reason, and that the cosmic plan has designs for me much grander than even those that I have conceived."
>
> DEEPAK CHOPRA, *The Seven Spiritual Laws of Success*

You Will Need
- Sandalwood incense in a holder
- Matches or a lighter
- 2 sheets of paper
- A pen, pencil, or marker
- A cauldron or earthenware flowerpot
- A small carnelian, fire agate, or fire opal
- Your book of shadows

Directions

1. Set the incense on your altar or other workspace and light it.

2. On one piece of paper, list the beliefs, behaviors, fears, habits, etc. that you feel are limiting you and causing you unhappiness. Your list may be as short or as long as you need it to be. You can write down all the things you intend to get rid of or just a few that are most important to eliminate at this time.

3. On the other piece of paper, list the opportunities you intend to attract, that you feel will make you happier and more fulfilled. These may be relationships, work-related possibilities, financial situations, attitude changes, lifestyle shifts, etc. Your list may be as short or as long as you need it to be. You can write down all the things you wish to create for yourself or just a few that are most important to you at this time.

4. When you've finished, read through the first list. Take a few moments to contemplate each thing on your list, how it came to be part of your life, what purpose it has served in the past, and why you now choose to eliminate it.

5. When you feel ready, light the first piece of paper and drop it into the cauldron or flowerpot. You may notice the fire spirits nearby, participating in the ritual.

6. As the paper burns, sense the unwanted ideas, conditions, etc. burning up too. Feel yourself letting go of old conceptions and limitations, releasing the burdens you've struggled with in the past. You might sense yourself growing lighter, freer, more optimistic. You could even experience a twinge of anxiety or sadness as these familiar things are purged from your life. Pay attention to your feelings and honor them.

7. When the paper has finished burning, read what you've written on the second sheet of paper. Take a few moments to contemplate each thing on your list, why you've chosen to bring it into your life, how you think it may change you for the better, and what you are willing to do to make this possibility a reality.

8. When you feel ready, light the second piece of paper and drop it into the cauldron or flowerpot. The womb-like shape of the cauldron or pot represents fertility and birth.

9. As the paper burns, the smoke carries your wishes to the spirit realm. Sense new opportunities coming to you. Envision yourself enjoying the newfound happiness, confidence, freedom, excitement, hope, comfort—whatever you intend to happen. You may also experience some apprehension as you embark on a new course and move into unknown territory. Pay attention to your feelings and honor them.

10. When the paper has finished burning, scatter the ashes beneath a tree.

11. Leave the gemstone for the fire spirits who have assisted you.

12. In your book of shadows, record your experience and the results.

13. Repeat this ritual whenever you feel a need to do so. As you progress, you may choose to release more old stuff and/or to bring additional things into your life. If it seems appropriate, invite fairy helpers to assist you.

JOURNEY TO FAIRYLAND WITH A GATEWAY CRYSTAL

Each crystal is unique and special, a distinctive life-form as individual as each human being is. Their shapes, colors, inclusions, and so on give crystals certain properties and abilities. Some crystals contain internal or external shapes that look like doors or windows. In rare instances, you might see what appears to be a stairway. A crystal with these types of portals is called a gateway crystal. You can work with a gateway crystal to access knowledge and magick from other civilizations, past or future. Gateway crystals provide entrance to the angelic realms, the devic kingdom, and the fairy world. Crystals that contain galaxies can lead you to different star systems. Some metaphysicians believe that adept crystal workers of Lemuria and Atlantis journeyed physically through the portals of large gateway crystals positioned in temples for that very purpose.

You Will Need

- A gateway crystal
- Your book of shadows
- Several small crystals

Directions

1. Silence all distractions. Turn off your phone, TV, etc. Close pets away where they won't bother you. If you live with other people, instruct them not to disturb you. This journey can take a half hour or longer.

2. Sit in a comfortable place. Relax and take several slow, deep breaths to calm your mind.

3. Hold the gateway crystal with both hands. Spend a few minutes communing with it, perhaps stroking its surface or sensing its resonance. If this is a crystal you've worked with before, it shouldn't take long to make the connection. If it's a new crystal for you, take as much time as you need to feel you've developed a bond with it.

4. Tell the crystal what you'd like it to do and ask for its assistance. You may speak aloud to it or mentally convey your intention to the crystal. Wait until you sense its agreement before continuing.

5. Visually examine the crystal. What sort of portals do you see in it? Markings that resemble windows or doorways may appear on the surface of the crystal, on its sides or faces, or inside—or all of these places.

6. Choose one of these portals and focus your attention on it. As you gaze at the portal, feel your awareness being drawn into the crystal. It's as if a door has opened and you've been invited to enter.

7. As you move deeper into the crystal, in imagination and spirit, you may notice fairies and other entities nearby. Perhaps you'll experience a tingling sensation. You may see sparkling light. You might even hear the fairies singing, for the fae love music.

8. Allow yourself to be drawn in deeper and deeper, until suddenly you realize you are no longer in the crystal—you've been transported beyond the physical realm to fairyland.

9. Gently slip into the land of the fae. Allow your awareness to expand to take in the immense place in which you now find yourself. What do you see? Hear? Feel? Smell? Some people see incredibly beautiful light that, despite its brilliance, doesn't hurt their eyes. Everything glows with this amazing light, yet it seems to have no source. You might see magnificent castles or lush landscapes rich with exotic flowers in colors more vibrant than anything you've ever seen on earth. What you witness may be in constant flux, emerging, dissolving, transforming as you watch. Resist the urge to analyze, comprehend, or quantify—just be open to whatever you experience.

10. Turn your attention to the inhabitants of this wondrous place: the fairies. What do they look like? What are they doing? Have you met any of these beings before in your meditations, spell-work, or dreams? Do you notice various sorts of fairies or only one type? How do they behave toward you—are they welcoming or standoffish?

11. If the fae folk invite you to join in their activities—and if you feel comfortable doing so—go for it. Remember the caveat discussed earlier in this book, however: Don't eat or drink with them. Some sources say you shouldn't dance with them either.

12. At some stage in your visit, you may choose to ask the fairies to share their wisdom with you. Most fairies possess healing skill, so you might seek information about how to treat an illness or request general advice. In the past, witches were believed to have gained their knowledge of healing from the fairies. The fae can also assist you in developing your psychic abilities, creative talent, and much more.

13. Remain in fairyland for as long as you like. Be careful, however, not to succumb to the seductiveness of this magickal realm. Legends abound with tales of people who became so enamored of this wondrous place that they never returned from the world of the fae.

14. When you're ready, thank the fairies for letting you visit their home and for whatever wisdom they've shared with you.

15. Cast your gaze about until you spot a window or door that leads into the gateway crystal. Pass through this portal and enter the crystal. In reverse order, follow the path that brought you to fairyland, back to your ordinary level of awareness. You may experience a sense of heaviness or a slowing of your thought processes as you move through the crystal and emerge once again into earth-consciousness.

16. Take a few minutes to reorient yourself. Thank the crystal for serving as your vehicle for journeying.

17. Record your experience and insights in your book of shadows.

18. Leave the small crystals for the fairies to thank them.

VISUALIZATION TO RELIEVE ANXIETY

It's natural to feel anxious at times when you're facing a challenge or encountering a situation that's outside your comfort zone. Growth often brings with it apprehension, discomfort, and fear of the unknown—consider the birth experience. When your heart starts to race, your stomach ties itself in knots, do this ritual to ground and center yourself. You may wish to call upon an animal spirit for help; for example, a fairy fox for cleverness, a cat *sidhe* for grace under pressure, or a spirit horse for strength and speed.

You Will Need
- Food for the wild animals

Directions
1. Take several slow, deep breaths. Sense your spirit animal helper nearby, giving you extra energy.

2. Count five things you can see right now. Focus your attention on each one for a few moments as you continue breathing slowly, deeply.

3. Next, count four things you can touch right now. Focus your attention on each one for a few moments as you continue breathing slowly, deeply.

4. Count three things you can hear right now. Focus your attention on each one for a few moments as you continue breathing slowly, deeply.

5. Count two things you can smell right now. Focus your attention on each one for a few moments as you continue breathing slowly, deeply.

6. Think of one thing that gives you comfort—your pet, taking a walk, sipping a cup of tea, for instance.

7. Continue breathing slowly and deeply until the anxiety diminishes.

8. Thank the fairy animal for its help. As soon as you can, set out food for the wild animals as a gift.

> "Believe in yourself. You are braver than you think, more talented than you know, and capable of more than you imagine."
>
> ROY T. BENNETT, *The Light in the Heart*

USE A MAGICK SQUARE FOR PERSONAL AND SPIRITUAL GROWTH

A magick square is an ancient configuration of smaller, numbered squares arranged in rows and columns in such a way that the numbers in each column and row add up to the same sum. Each design corresponds to one of the celestial bodies in our solar system. One of the simplest squares, which magick workers associate with the planet Saturn, consists of nine small squares within a larger one. You can use magick squares in various ways for spellcraft (my book *The Modern Witchcraft Grimoire* shows you how to create sigils on the square). This one incorporates the power of crystals to support your intentions. You may wish to ask the fairies to participate—which ones you invite will depend on the nature of your intentions.

You Will Need

- A magick square
- A piece of paper
- A pen, pencil, or marker
- 10 clear quartz crystals or 10 gemstones
- A piece of black cloth

Directions

1. Lay the magick square faceup on your altar or another flat surface, where it can remain overnight. You may download the image from the Internet. If you think you'll use this tool regularly, you might want to draw it on a piece of wood, foam core board, or fabric.

2. On the paper, list nine things that you feel will foster your personal or spiritual growth. For example, you might want to be kinder and more compassionate, to do volunteer work for a cause you believe in, to be more consistent in your magickal practice— whatever you consider important.

3. When you've finished the list, assign each intention to a crystal or gemstone. If you decide to use gemstones for this spell, select stones that relate to your purpose. For instance, rose quartz for emotional balance, bloodstone for courage, or star sapphire for clarity of purpose. (See the Appendix for lists of correspondences.)

4. Set each crystal or gemstone on a square. As you position each stone, state your intention aloud and imagine yourself actualizing it.

5. When you've finished placing all nine crystals or gemstones on the magick square, cover everything with the black cloth and say aloud: "So MOTE IT BE." Let everything remain in place overnight.

6. Leave the tenth crystal or gemstone for the fairy who helped you as a thank-you gift.

VISIT THE OTHERWORLD TO EASE GRIEF

Death of the physical body is inevitable, and we'll all lose loved ones at some time in our lives. Knowing they're not gone from us forever—and that we can visit them on the Other Side—can help to ease the pain we suffer. The Irish *bean sidhe*, or banshee, may seem like a frightening figure in myths, but she's a knowledgeable guide if you choose to travel to the world of spirit. If you are nearing the time of transition yourself, a preliminary journey to check out your future home may calm anxiety about passing over. Don't worry, you won't get stuck there—you won't travel physically, and you can come back whenever you please.

You Will Need

- A pentagram or protection amulet, such as the one described in Chapter 8
- A silver charm shaped like a crescent moon
- Your book of shadows

Directions

1. Silence all distractions. Turn off your phone, TV, music, etc. Close pets away where they won't bother you. If you live with other people, instruct them not to disturb you. This journey can take a half hour or longer.

2. Before you begin, set your intention. If you want to meet a particular being, send out a mental greeting and ask that entity to welcome you.

3. Hold/wear the pentagram or protection amulet.

4. Sit in a comfortable place. Close your eyes and envision yourself surrounded by a ball of pure white light, while you say aloud:

   "I AM PROTECTED BY DIVINE WHITE LIGHT, NOW AND ALWAYS."

5. Take several slow, deep breaths as you feel yourself relaxing, your mind growing quiet. Invite a *bean sidhe* to serve as your psychic tour guide.

6. Envision your aura gradually expanding in all directions, until you sense it extending a couple feet out from your physical body. Then mentally pull it back closer to you, so that it feels like it's only about 6 inches thick.

7. Repeat this two more times, and each time expand your aura farther.

8. When you feel ready, imagine an inner part of yourself rising up to the crown chakra at the top of your head. Allow this part of you to continue rising, until you sense you are floating near the ceiling. Look down and observe your physical body sitting comfortably and safely below.

9. Envision yourself sliding easily through the ceiling, until you are hovering above your home (or wherever you began this journey). From this elevated vantage point, look around at trees, buildings, and other familiar things. If you feel apprehensive or nervous, notice the *bean sidhe* is at your side—she's made this trip countless times and can guide you safely.

10. Continue floating higher and higher, until you sense yourself entering a realm of light, peace, and joy. You may see radiant colors, hear exquisite music, or something else. Let the *bean sidhe* lead you deeper into this blissful realm.

11. You may sense beings there who are familiar to you. Notice that you can communicate with these beings telepathically. If you've asked someone in particular to meet you, you may experience this entity's presence nearby. Feel love and joy flowing between you. Observe the peace and happiness your loved ones here are enjoying.

12. Explore this wondrous world for as long as you like. Talk with the entities there, both those you knew on earth and those who may never have incarnated. Ask questions, and you'll receive answers.

13. When you are ready, choose to return to earth. Set the intention that you will remember all you've experienced in this other realm.

14. Gently descend to the physical plane again. Comfortably reenter your corporeal body, feeling relaxed and peaceful.

15. Take a few minutes to reorient yourself, then open your eyes.

16. Leave the silver charm for the *bean sidhe* as a thank-you gift.

17. Record your experiences in your book of shadows.

Chapter 12

WORKING WITH FAIRIES ON SABBATS AND HOLIDAYS

C eltic Wiccans and neopagans celebrate eight major holidays, or "sabbats," one every six weeks. Together, they compose what's known as the Wheel of the Year. The wheel has its roots in the old agricultural festivals that marked the beginnings, endings, and peaks of the seasons in Britain, Ireland, and Europe.

Four of the holidays relate to the four great Celtic/Irish fire festivals. Called the "cross-quarter" days, because they mark the midpoints of the seasons, these festivals are Samhain, Imbolc, Beltane, and Lughnasadh. The four solar festivals—Yule (winter solstice), Ostara (spring equinox), Midsummer or Litha (summer solstice), and Mabon (fall equinox)—celebrate the dates when the sun enters 0 degrees of the cardinal signs of the zodiac: Capricorn, Aries, Cancer, and Libra, respectively. These high-energy days bring opportunities for performing special holiday spells and rituals. In this chapter you'll find a spell, ritual, blessing, meditation, journey, or other practice suitable to enact on each of these sabbats.

FAIRIES AND SABBATS

Which fairies might you like to invite to your sabbat celebrations? Which ones have traditionally been associated with the holidays? Which ones can bring positive energy, wisdom, healing, guidance, and other gifts to you on these special days?

- **BEAN SIDHES:** This sometimes frightening fairy that folklore associates with death is a frequent flier between the earth plane and the world of spirits. She's also linked with Samhain and the winter season, when crops die and the earth sleeps (in the northern hemisphere). Usually depicted as a ghostly female elder, she can connect you with the spirits of loved ones on the Other Side, as you learned in the previous chapter, and help you overcome fear of your own passing. A *bean sidhe* can also guide you through major life transitions that scare you.

- **PIXIES:** These nature guardians could be welcome guests at any sabbat celebration because the holidays recognize and honor nature's cycles. Because of their creative energy, however, we often associate them with the fertile spring and summer months, as well as the sabbats that witches mark during the warmer half of the year: Beltane, Ostara, and Midsummer.

- **ELVES:** Hardworking, skillful, and practical elves can show you how to use your talents productively. They can also help you get organized, prepare for the future, and become more efficient. In agrarian cultures, autumn is a season of working hard to bring in the harvest in preparation for the long, bleak months ahead. Consequently, witches link elves with this time of the year, at Lughnasadh and Mabon, even though fairy tales and contemporary Western culture connect them with the Christmas season.

- **ELEMENTAL FAIRIES:** Witches associate the four elements with the four seasons of the year. The element of air relates to spring. Fire correlates with summer. Water corresponds to autumn, and earth to winter. You may want to consider these connections when working with elemental fairies at different times of the year.

SAMHAIN SPELL TO COMMUNICATE WITH LOVED ONES ON THE OTHER SIDE

Fairies can move with ease between the physical and nonphysical worlds. Therefore, they can help you connect with your loved ones who no longer reside on earth and have gone over to the Other Side. The veil that separates the seen and unseen worlds is thinnest on Samhain (usually celebrated on the night of October 31), so this is a good time to commune with spirits of all kinds. The *bean sidhe*, who know the time and place when someone will leave this world, can help you prepare for a loved one's passing.

You Will Need

- A gift of food for the *bean sidhe*
- Your book of shadows

Directions

1. Sit in a comfortable place where you won't be disturbed. Silence your phone, TV, and other distractions.

2. Close your eyes and envision yourself surrounded by a ball of pure white light, while you say aloud:

    "I AM PROTECTED BY DIVINE WHITE LIGHT, IN ALL SITUATIONS, NOW AND ALWAYS."

3. Take several slow, deep breaths as you feel yourself relaxing, your mind growing quiet. Ask the *bean sidhe* for assistance. If you've established a relationship with a different fairy guardian, ask that fairy to serve as your guide.

4. Bring to mind an image of the loved one you want to contact. If you wish, call the person's name. (Note: Sometimes another spirit who once lived on this planet will come through instead with a message for you. Remain open to hearing what this entity has to share with you.)

5. You may notice a tingling sensation at the top of your head or at your heart center, or someplace else, as if the person's spirit were lightly touching you. Perhaps you'll feel a chill run up your spine,

smell a favorite scent that person wore while on earth, or sense the person's presence. If you're lucky, you might even see your loved one's etheric image. Spirits make themselves known in myriad ways. As you grow familiar with this type of communication, you may find that your loved ones use different methods to let you know when they're around.

6. When you feel your loved one is nearby, mentally ask for insight, guidance, or reassurance that life doesn't end when the physical body dies but continues in another form—or many forms— forever. If you have a specific question, ask it. Most likely, you'll intuit a response rather than actually hearing it spoken aloud, although that can happen. The response may come as an instantaneous *knowing* instead of in complete sentences. (Note: Don't be surprised if the spirit conveys a message that isn't what you asked for. Accept it for your wisdom and growth. Even if it doesn't make sense at the time, it probably will later on.)

7. Ask for a sign that will let you know whenever your loved one is near. I often see bright red cardinals when my deceased partner's spirit is present.

8. Continue for as long as you wish. When you feel tired, lose your focus, or intuit that your loved one is ready to end the session, slowly open your eyes. Thank the spirit(s) with whom you've connected and request another meeting in the future.

9. Thank the *bean sidhe* who helped you in this endeavor, and offer a gift of food to show your appreciation.

10. In your book of shadows, write down what you experienced.

BURN A YULE FIRE FOR GOOD FORTUNE

The ancient Irish wise men and women known as the Druids revered trees and understood their magickal natures, as we discussed in Chapter 4. About twenty different trees were considered sacred (depending on whose perspective you take), and each tree was believed to have its own unique properties. Oaks, for instance, symbolize strength and longevity. Traditionally, an oak log forms the centerpiece of a Yule fire burned on the winter solstice. If you wish, you can combine several different types of wood in a ritual fire to produce a desired effect. Before you cut a twig or branch from a tree, ask the tree's permission and thank it afterward.

You Will Need

- An oak log
- Small pieces of wood, twigs, bark, etc. (these may be oak or other types of wood)
- Fireplace or fire pit
- A piece of paper
- A pen, pencil, or marker
- Matches or a lighter
- Gifts of food and drink for the fairies (milk, mead, holiday cookies, fruitcake)
- 1 or more leather drawstring pouches

Directions

1. Lay the oak log and other bits of wood in a fireplace, fire pit, or other spot where they can burn safely. If you saved a piece of last year's Yule log, add it too.

2. Respectfully invite woodland fairies to join you in celebrating.

3. On the piece of paper, write wishes you hope will come true in the coming year. Fold the paper three times.

4. Light the fire. As it burns, you may see fairies from the fire element, known as salamanders, dancing in the flames.

5. Drop the paper with your wishes on it into the flames. Ask the fairies to carry your hopes and dreams into the realm of magick, where they can bring their influence to bear and help your wishes manifest.

6. While the fire burns, you may choose to sing, dance, or eat and drink special holiday foods/beverages, such as hot mulled cider or wine, in front of it. You may notice the fairies dancing along

with you. Share the food you've prepared with them, but don't eat anything they offer to you.

7. Save a piece of the Yule log to burn in next year's ritual fire.

8. When the fire has burned down completely and the ashes have cooled, scoop some into a pouch as a good luck talisman for the coming year. You may want to make additional talismans for friends and loved ones.

9. Sprinkle the remaining ashes outside at the base of a tree or in another place in nature where you sense the presence of woodland fairies. Thank them for their assistance and wish them well.

The Sun King's Journey

Pagan mythology describes the apparent passage of the sun through the heavens each year as the journey of the Sun King, who drives his shining chariot across the sky. In pre-Christian Europe and Britain, the winter solstice celebrated the Sun King's birth. This beloved deity brought light into the world during the darkest time of all.

IMBOLC CANDLE SPELL FOR INSPIRATION

Witches celebrate Imbolc, or Brigid's Day, between the evening of January 31 and February 2. Imbolc is also known as Candlemas, so it's traditional to light candles on this holiday. This spell sparks your imagination and fires up your creative power. Invite the fire fairies known as salamanders to join you.

You Will Need

- 3 orange taper candles
- Patchouli or cinnamon essential oil
- Candleholders
- Matches or a lighter
- A tarot card from the suit of Wands
- 1 or more fire agates

Directions

1. Anoint each candle with essential oil. Don't put oil on the wicks.

2. Fit the candles into their holders and set them on your altar, table, or another flat surface. Configure them in a triangular pattern, so that each candle is 6 inches away from the others. Triangles symbolize action and movement in a designated direction.

3. Light the candles. As the flames spark to life, sense the presence of the salamanders that you've invited to join you. Feel the energy in the room brightening, quickening, crackling with vitality. It may even seem to grow warmer as you continue working.

4. If you're looking for a new creative project, choose the Ace of Wands from a tarot deck. If you feel a need for more power or creative control in a venture, select the Queen of Wands (women) or the King of Wands (men). If you seek inspiration after a setback or dry spell, pick the Nine of Wands, sometimes thought of as the "recovery card." Lay the tarot card faceup in the center of the triangular configuration of candles.

5. Set the fire agate(s) on top of the tarot card. Fire agates are associated with the sacral chakra, the body's energy center that resonates with creative vitality.

6. Envision your hopes and dreams manifesting in a joyful way that benefits all concerned. See yourself in the position you desire, accomplishing the goal you've set for yourself, receiving recognition and rewards, etc.

7. Let the candles burn down completely. (Caution: Don't leave burning candles unattended.)

8. Return the tarot card to its deck.

9. Leave the fire agate on your altar as a gift for the salamanders— one day you'll notice the stone has disappeared. Alternately, you can put the agate in a special place where you think the fairies will find it.

Goddess of the Hearth and Forge

Brigid's association with the fires of the hearth and the forge represents the strengthening of the sun's light, as well as the union of feminine and masculine energies that constitute creativity in the material world. Brigid is one of the fertility goddesses, and Imbolc means "in the belly." This holiday honors all forms of creativity, of the mind as well as the body. Illustrations of Brigid sometimes show her stirring a great cauldron, the witch's magick tool that symbolizes the womb and the receptive, fertile nature of the Divine Feminine.

DANCE AROUND A MAYPOLE ON BELTANE

Witches usually celebrate Beltane on May 1. The second fertility holiday in the Wheel of the Year, it coincides with a time of fruitfulness and beauty on earth, and honors all of nature. The ancient tradition of dancing around a Maypole symbolizes the sexual aspect of this sabbat. You can enjoy this age-old practice with a group of fellow witches or friends—invite the nature fairies, who love music and dancing, to join you too.

You Will Need
- Real or artificial flowers
- A measuring tape
- Florist's wire
- Scissors
- Tape
- A wooden pole about 8 feet long
- Multicolored ribbons, each about 10 to 12 feet long
- Music
- Food and drink for the participants and for the fairies

Directions
1. Use real or artificial flowers (artificial ones are easier to work with and will last longer) to make a floral headdress to wear while you dance around the Maypole.

2. Measure a length of flexible florist's wire that will fit around your head and cut the wire. Tape the ends of the wire together to form a circle.

3. Arrange the flowers on the wire in a design you like, and then secure them in place with the tape to form a pretty headpiece.

4. Tie the ribbons, one for each participant, to one end of the pole.

5. Mount the pole outdoors in a place where you will have plenty of room to dance around it.

6. Each participant in the dance holds the end of a ribbon. All stand in a circle around the Maypole. Dancers face in opposite directions so that person A dances in a clockwise direction, person B dances counterclockwise, person C dances clockwise, and so on.

7. Play lively Celtic music.

8. Begin dancing as described above. As you dance, alternate holding your ribbon up so that the person next to you can duck under it, and then you'll duck under the ribbon held by the next person as you circle around the pole. You may sense the fairies dancing along with you. (If you like, you can view this ritual online before trying it yourself.) Feel free to add other steps if you wish—the dance can be as simple or complex as you like.

9. As you dance, the ribbons wrap around the Maypole, creating a colorful interwoven pattern that signifies the interwoven nature of our lives on earth.

10. At the end of the dance, tie the ribbons at the bottom of the pole.

11. According to tradition, a woman who seeks a lover tosses her headdress over the top of the Maypole, which symbolizes the sex act, and asks the Goddess to bring her a partner. Any women in the group who wish to petition the Goddess for partners can do this now.

12. Share food and drink with fellow celebrants—and leave some for the fairies to enjoy.

CELEBRATE LIFE OVER DEATH ON OSTARA

Pagans and witches celebrate Ostara on the first day of spring, around March 21. In the northern hemisphere, the spring equinox ushers in warmer weather, days that are longer than nights, and life reawakening. Ostara gets its name from the German fertility goddess Ostare; therefore rituals on this sabbat often celebrate fertility of the mind and/or body. The holiday also recognizes the triumph of life over death. Invite the nature spirits to participate in this ritual.

You Will Need

- An egg-dyeing kit
- Hard-boiled eggs, 1 for each friend, family member, or loved one you choose to gift, plus 1 (or more) for the fairies
- A marker that will write on the eggshells
- Hard-boiled eggs to place on graves

Directions

1. Dye the eggs according to the instructions on the kit. Eggs represent fertility/creativity, promise, new life, and beginnings.

2. Look online for pictures of the Ogham alphabet. On the eggs you plan to give to friends, family members, and other loved ones, draw the Ogham rune birch/*beth*, which represents new beginnings and opportunities. If you like, you may draw other images too, or write good wishes for the people to whom you will give the eggs.

3. In earlier times, people placed eggs on graves as a sign to those on the Other Side that rebirth follows physical death. Perhaps this signified a belief in reincarnation. On the eggs you've chosen for this purpose, write the Ogham letter willow/*saille*, which signifies communication with spirits.

4. Go to a cemetery and lay the eggs on graves. These may be the graves of loved ones you knew in this lifetime or of people you wish to honor even if you weren't acquainted with them personally.

5. Leave one or more eggs for the fairies as a gift.

MAKE A MIDSUMMER INVISIBILITY AMULET

Have you ever wanted to be invisible? This amulet protects you against prying eyes, nosy neighbors, enemies, or anyone else that you don't want to know your business. Don't worry, you won't physically disappear. Instead, you will erect a magick veil that will hide you temporarily, until you choose to be seen again.

You Will Need

- Fern seeds
- A black drawstring pouch made of silk or another natural material
- Basil incense
- An incense burner (optional)
- Matches or a lighter
- Milk and honey for the sprites who help you
- String or ribbon (optional)

Directions

1. Invite the nature fairies known as sprites to assist you in working this spell. Speak respectfully to them and thank them for taking care of earth's plant life.

2. At midnight on Midsummer's Eve, collect fern seeds. Herbs gathered now are believed to have unparalleled potency. Thank the ferns for giving up their seeds.

3. Put the seeds in the pouch and tie it shut.

4. Light the incense—basil is an herb witches use for protection. If you're burning stick incense, you can hold the stick in one hand and slowly move it up, down, and around your body so that the smoke envelops you from head to toe. Hold the pouch in your other hand.

5. If you're using an incense burner, fit the incense in it and light the incense. Set the burner on the floor and stand beside it, turning slowly in the drifting smoke so that it touches you on all sides.

6. Thank the sprites for their assistance. Set a bowl of milk and honey outside for them to show your appreciation.

7. Put the amulet pouch in your pocket, or fasten a string, ribbon, etc. to it and wear it around your neck.

8. Before you go out into the world, visualize a black veil covering you from head to foot, enabling you to move about in complete secrecy. Remove the veil when you're ready to be seen again.

BAKE MAGICK BREAD ON LUGHNASADH

Baking bread is a time-honored tradition on Lughnasadh. Instead of just making ordinary bread, infuse it with magick—this is a perfect example of kitchen witchery. To do this, set your intention beforehand, then select ingredients that correspond to what you desire. For instance, if your goal is to attract prosperity, bake whole-wheat bread. To get a job or improve conditions in your workplace, oatmeal is a good choice. Bread with walnuts in it (such as pumpkin or banana bread) can benefit mental abilities and communication. Cinnamon bread encourages friendship, and garlic bread boosts courage. Brownies are known to pitch in with domestic tasks, so you may want to invite them to join you.

You Will Need
- A piece of paper
- A pen, pencil, marker, or other writing tool
- Ingredients for the recipe you've chosen
- Tools needed to make the recipe you've chosen: a large bowl, wooden spoons, measuring cups, baking pans, etc.

Directions
1. Spend some time determining exactly what you want to achieve with this spell. Then write an affirmation that states your intention. Keep it short, precise, and positive, and word it in the present

tense as if the condition you desire already exists. For example: "I now have a job that is perfect for me in every way."

2. Throughout the process, repeat your affirmation aloud regularly. Envision the end result you desire and mentally project the image into the dough as you mix, knead, etc. You may sense the fairies standing beside you in the kitchen, sitting on the counter or dipping their fingers in the batter.

3. Eat the finished bread, alone or with friends, knowing that with each bite you are nourishing your intention and bringing it into manifestation.

4. Be sure to share the magick bread with your fairy helpers and thank them for assisting you.

> "Come up here, O dusty feet!
> Here is fairy bread to eat.
> Here in my retiring room,
> Children, you may dine
> On the golden smell of broom
> And the shade of pine;
> And when you have eaten well,
> Fairy stories hear and tell."
>
> ROBERT LOUIS STEVENSON, author and poet

DRAW A TRISKELE ON MABON TO FIND BALANCE

The Celtic triple spiral known as a triskele symbolizes the earth, sea, and sky. Therefore, it shows the harmonious relationship between these regions and reminds us to bring ourselves into balance with nature. The triskele also represents life, death, and rebirth. On this day of the autumn equinox, as you stand on the threshold between summer and winter, use this image to meditate on the ongoing cycle of existence. Because fairies live practically forever, they can help you understand that although human bodies die, our souls are immortal. Invite the nature fairies to join you.

You Will Need

- A piece of paper
- Felt-tip marker(s)
- Food for the fairies

Directions

1. On the piece of paper, draw a triskele (taken from an image online). It may be as large or as small as you choose.

2. While you work, keep your attention focused on the image you are drawing. Release other thoughts and let your mind grow calm, as you contemplate your connection with All That Is. If you like, you can draw the symbol large enough that you can stand in the center of it.

3. When you've finished, place the symbol on your altar or in another place where you'll see it often. Whenever you feel upset or out of sorts, look at the triskele and remind yourself that you are in harmony with Divine Will and at one with the universe.

4. Alternately, you can draw a temporary triskele outdoors on the ground with a stick or with chalk on pavement. Allow the symbol to wear away naturally—you can always draw another. Or, you can make a permanent one by configuring stones in the triple spiral pattern.

5. Leave food for the fairies as a thank-you gift.

Chapter 13

TAKING THE NEXT STEP

Today's world is one in which we're becoming more and more estranged from nature, where our attention is focused on the material plane and disconnected from the spiritual one. Technology plays an increasingly important role in our everyday affairs, while imagination, intuition, and intimacy with the Divine are being relegated to the realm of fantasy. At the same time, however, Wicca and witchcraft are gaining popularity worldwide, partly as a reaction to contemporary society's dependence on electronic devices, artificial intelligence, and pharmaceuticals.

Human beings need spiritual "food" to thrive. Following a spiritual path doesn't mean you have to dissociate yourself from technology; it just means you don't let it rule your life. It's all about balance. I play music on my cell phone and listen to the Dalai Lama chant on *YouTube*. But I also spend time meditating, doing yoga, walking outdoors, communing with spirits, reading paper books, and playing with my cat.

WITCHES AND THE FAE

Those of us who follow the Way of the Witch are fortunate to enjoy a closer connection with nature and the spirit world than most people do. A lot of us use botanicals and crystals in our spellwork. We harmonize our activities with lunar and solar cycles. We honor deities and engage with them in our rituals. And some of us interact with fairies.

Relationships between witches and fairies aren't new. Centuries ago, people believed that witches learned their craft from the fae—and perhaps they did. Today, many of us are once again turning to these spirit helpers for insight, guidance, and information that will further our magickal practice. In so doing, we may build a bridge between the past and the future, ultimately benefiting not only ourselves but the world as well.

GOING FORWARD IN YOUR WORK WITH THE FAE

Throughout this book we've talked about ways to attract and work with fairies. Fairy Witchcraft and Faery Wicca bear many similarities to witchy paths you may already be familiar with, but they also emphasize some things that aren't so significant in other branches of the Craft of the Wise. According to Morgan Daimler, author of *Fairycraft*, "At heart [Fairy Witchcraft] is a wild and experiential path that encourages the witch to learn how to safely reach out to the Otherworld and to take chances to create connections to Fairy which involve risk balanced with wisdom."

If you've chosen to embark on this path, see yourself as an adventurer trekking into territory that may be unfamiliar to you but that offers untold riches. Like adventurers in the past, you have the opportunity and perhaps a responsibility to bring back the knowledge you glean from your travels, so that everyone may benefit.

Journey to Fairyland and Elsewhere

In your practice as a witch, you may have had occasion to explore other realms of existence. If you decide to delve deeper into the world of the fae, you'll probably take many trips to the Otherworld and Underworld (see Chapter 4). Only there can you gain firsthand knowledge of their habitat, lifestyles, customs, relationships, and behaviors. The land of the fae is simultaneously more subtle and more intense than our own, so your experiences there will be of a different nature altogether.

R.J. Stewart, author of *Earth Light, Power Within the Land,* and numerous other books, agrees with other fairy researchers that "The faery realm is the Primal Land: wherever you are, whatever land you are in, the faery realm is the primal image of that land...our world is devolved or reflected *out of* the primal image of the faery world." In short, the land of the fae is the prototype for everything we know on earth. If that's the case, learning about it directly from the fae will teach you about humankind's origins, our place in the cosmos, and the purpose of earthly incarnation. Here you'll gain an entirely different perspective about evolution from what you learned in science class!

Chapter 11 offers suggestions and instructions for journeying to fairyland as well as to other places beyond our own planet. You'll also find techniques for spiritual journeying—walking between the worlds—in the writings of many shamans from various cultures and traditions. If you establish a relationship with a particular fairy, you may travel with this companion known as a co-walker. I urge you to at least give it a try. Over the years, I've safely journeyed to many places beyond earth and gained precious knowledge in these places that I couldn't have learned any other way.

Study Myths

In Bill Moyers's discussions with mythologist Joseph Campbell on the TV series *The Power of Myth*, he described myths as being "stories of our search...through the ages for meaning, for significance, to make life signify, to touch the eternal, to understand the mysterious, to find out who we are." Campbell himself defined myths as "clues to the spiritual potentialities of the human life....The experience of *life*."

All cultures, all religions and belief systems have myths that connect people to Source. And despite the common definition of "myth" as falsehood, in reality myths are vast reservoirs of great truths that can only be conveyed through the vehicles of symbol and story. Myths, legends, and folklore frequently discuss spirit beings who possess superhuman abilities, magickal powers, and knowledge far beyond that of mortals.

The contemporary paths known as Fairy Witchcraft and Faery Wicca draw upon the ancient myths of the Celtic people, their history, deities, beliefs, practices, holidays, etc. It's helpful to study these myths in order to understand the age-old concepts on which our modern interpretations are based. I recommend looking deeper into the myths of the fairy families discussed in Chapter 2: the Tuatha dé Danann, the Seelie and Unseelie Courts, and the Tylwyth Teg. These ancient traditions help to ground us in our present-day practices as witches and provide perspective regarding our history. To ignore them would be akin to studying Christianity and skipping Adam and Eve, or examining American history and omitting the Pilgrims. For the record, though, the paths of Fairy Witchcraft and Faery Wicca aren't specifically cultural or denominational.

Strengthen Your Relationship with Nature

Throughout this book I've stressed the importance of working with nature and the fairies who serve as guardians to the plants and animals on our planet. This may be the most vital aspect of partnering with the fae now, in magickal work and in our everyday lives. Ultimately, I think Mother Earth will do just fine without human beings occupying her terrain, but our species is in danger if we don't get our act together. Therefore, as you take the next steps into developing your relationship with the fae, your commitment to this objective and your efforts to support a better environment for all species will be important for the future of our lives on this planet.

In his book *Knowledge of the Higher Worlds and Its Attainment*, Austrian philosopher and metaphysician Rudolf Steiner, who founded anthroposophy and the Waldorf Schools, recommended communing with plants as a way to gain spiritual wisdom. Practice focusing your attention on a plant, while silencing your preconceptions so that you can sense the plant's innate intelligence. In this way, you connect with the spirits or devas that inhabit the plant and that inspire its growth. You may see the plant glowing, exhibiting its inner radiance. You may intuit messages from the plant and its resident fairy. Witches who do plant magick are familiar with the characteristics and properties of various botanicals. But when you devote yourself to developing a personal relationship with individual plants, you'll discover their true intent and power, directly from the source.

Hone Your Intuition

Fairies communicate intuitively, therefore if you want to develop a rapport with them you'll need to do it with thoughts and visions, not words. You can use words in chants, affirmations, incantations, etc. when working with the fae, but those are mostly for your benefit, to help deepen your focus and raise your energy.

Practice honing your intuition by engaging in exercises designed to strengthen your sixth sense.

- Pay attention to signs and hunches. If you get a hunch you should or shouldn't do something, follow it. If you notice an animal or bird in a place that's not typical for it, that could be a sign for you. Maybe you'll start seeing numbers, patterns, or words repeatedly—they might be signals. Your intuition slips messages to you all the time, and the more you practice awareness the clearer those messages will become.

- Try sensing what you can't see with your physical eyes. Use a deck of Zener cards, created by psychologist Karl Zener for ESP experiments, to develop your psychic skills. With a friend, practice sending and receiving the images on these cards telepathically. Or, ask a friend to put pictures from magazines in plain envelopes, without showing them to you, then try to intuit the pictures. How successful were you?

- Communicate telepathically with a pet. Animals have keenly developed intuitions and can pick up on your thoughts—notice how your cat hides when it's time to go to the vet, even before you get out her carrier. Practice sending visual messages to your pet— you may be surprised at how quickly Fluffy or Fido responds.

Listen to Children

Young children often see fairies where adults don't. That's partly because they haven't yet been indoctrinated to believe that only the physical world is real. Their minds are flexible and open, so they can see and hear and sense all kinds of things that we've blocked out. If a preschool-age child tells you she sees a fairy, ask her what it looks like. What is it doing? Why is it here and what does it want?

I encourage you to read other books about fairies and Fairy Witchcraft. Visit online sites, such as Fairyist.com. Talk to other witches and fairy enthusiasts about their experiences. Share your own experiences with others. For many years, this ancient knowledge has been shrouded in ignorance, skepticism, and misconceptions. Now it's time to revive the secrets our ancestors knew, for our growth as witches and for the benefit of all. Blessed be.

Appendix

GEMSTONES FOR SPELLS AND RITUALS

Gemstones for Love and Friendship
CARNELIAN: Stimulates passion and sexual desire
DIAMOND: Deepens commitment and trust in a love relationship
GARNET: Increases love and passion
OPAL: Aids love and seduction
PEARL: Encourages love, happiness, and emotional balance
QUARTZ (ROSE): Attracts romance, affection, and friendship

Gemstones for Prosperity and Abundance
AGATE (GREEN): Helps stabilize your finances
AVENTURINE: Attracts wealth and abundance
JADE: Brings luck and success in financial areas
QUARTZ ABUNDANCE CRYSTAL: Aids financial growth and attracts abundance of all kinds
TIGER'S EYE: Increases good fortune and prosperity

Gemstones for Protection
AMBER: Though not really a stone—it's fossilized sap—amber offers protection from physical or nonphysical threats
BLOODSTONE: Provides physical protection and bolsters courage; the ancients believed it stanched the flow of blood
ONYX: Gives you strength to stand up to your adversaries
PERIDOT: Repels negative energies and neutralizes toxins
SNOWFLAKE OBSIDIAN: Provides overall protection
TOURMALINE: Shields you from unwanted energies in the environment, such as EMFs

Gemstones for Health and Healing

AMETHYST: Increases relaxation

CHRYSOCOLLA: Eases emotional pain

CITRINE: Promotes cleansing and dissolves impurities

FLUORITE: Eases stress and stress-related problems

JADE: Supports good health and longevity

JASPER: Brown jasper supports physical healing; poppy jasper breaks up blockages that prevent energy from circulating through the body

Gemstones for Personal and Professional Success

HEMATITE: Deflects negativity, encourages determination, and promotes justice in legal matters

ONYX: Gives you strength to stand up to your adversaries

STAR SAPPHIRE: Strengthens hope and clarity of purpose

TOPAZ: Increases confidence and courage; attracts fame and financial success

Gemstones for Personal and Spiritual Growth

AQUAMARINE: Stimulates intuition, imagination, and creativity

FLUORITE: Improves concentration and mental clarity

LAPIS LAZULI: Deepens insight and inner wisdom

MOLDAVITE: Enhances your ability to communicate with spirits, deities, and extraterrestrials

OBSIDIAN: Provides strength to face obstacles; helps you break old habits

SAPPHIRE: Increases spiritual knowledge and connection with the Divine

FLOWERS FOR SPELLS AND RITUALS

Flowers for Love and Friendship

DAISY: Inspires playfulness in love and friendship

GERANIUM (ROSE-COLORED): Boosts fertility and love

JASMINE: Encourages love, harmony, seduction, and sensuality

MYRTLE: Brings luck in love

ROSE: Attracts love and friendship; pink for affection, red for passion

Flowers for Prosperity and Abundance

DAFFODIL: Attracts good luck

MARIGOLD: Encourages financial gain

SUNFLOWER: Its numerous seeds represent abundance, and its sunny yellow petals suggest gold

TULIP: The cuplike shape represents a vessel to hold money and treasures

Flowers for Protection

CARNATION (WHITE): Brings protection and strength

GERANIUM (WHITE): Helps protect you and your home

LILAC (WHITE): Offers general protection and banishes negative energy

LILY (WHITE): Repels and removes hexes; guards the soul as it journeys into the afterlife

SNAPDRAGON (WHITE): Protects you from illusion or deception; safeguards your home

Flowers for Health and Healing

CALENDULA: Soothes cuts and skin conditions

CHAMOMILE: Aids stomach problems; eases stress and supports relaxation

DANDELION: Contains iron; zinc; potassium; and vitamins A, B, C, and D

LAVENDER: Calms body, mind, and spirit, and encourages relaxation and sleep

Flowers for Personal and Professional Success

CLOVER: Attracts good luck

IRIS: The iris's three petals are said to symbolize faith, wisdom, and valor—qualities necessary to success

LILY OF THE VALLEY: Enhances concentration and mental ability

MARIGOLD: Encourages recognition; brings success in legal matters

Flowers for Personal and Spiritual Growth

CARNATION: Promotes strength and perseverance

ROSE (PINK): Increases self-love and acceptance

ROSE (YELLOW): Enhances creativity

SUNFLOWER: Boosts self-confidence

HERBS AND SPICES FOR SPELLS AND RITUALS

Herbs and Spices for Love and Friendship

CAYENNE: Sparks sexuality and desire

GINGER: Stimulates romance, excitement, and sexuality

MARJORAM: Blesses a new union and brings happiness

VANILLA: Encourages a more joyful and lighthearted approach to love

Herbs and Spices for Prosperity and Abundance

CINNAMON: Revs up the spell's power

DILL (SEED OR WEED): Attracts good fortune

MINT: One of the most popular, all-purpose money herbs

PARSLEY: Encourages prosperity and success

Herbs and Spices for Protection

ANGELICA: Use it magickally for protection and purification

BASIL: One of the most popular all-around protection herbs

CARAWAY (SEEDS): Protects you and your home from thieves

COMFREY: Provides protection while traveling

ROSEMARY: Provides safety and clears negative vibes

Herbs and Spices for Health and Healing

CHAMOMILE: Aids stomach problems; eases stress and supports relaxation

COMFREY: Encourages bone health and healing

GINGER: Improves digestion, calms nausea

PEPPERMINT: Aids digestion and heartburn, eases headaches

YARROW: In a poultice, it helps stanch bleeding

Herbs and Spices for Personal and Professional Success

ALLSPICE: Encourages prosperity and good luck

BAY (BAY LAUREL): Used to crown the victor of games in ancient Rome, it enhances success and wisdom

NETTLE: Mitigates thorny situations and shows you how to handle problems

NUTMEG: Brings success in financial ventures

Herbs and Spices for Personal and Spiritual Growth

MARJORAM: Encourages cooperation; supports life changes
SAGE: Improves memory, clears old attitudes
THYME: Strengthens focus and concentration
VERBENA: Increases skill in artistic areas, especially performance

ESSENTIAL OILS AND INCENSE FOR SPELLS AND RITUALS

Essential Oils and Incense for Love and Friendship

JASMINE: Encourages love, harmony, seduction, and sensuality
MUSK: Heightens sensuality and sexuality
PATCHOULI: Boosts passion and sensuality
ROSE: Attracts love and friendship
YLANG-YLANG: Increases sensuality and attractiveness

Essential Oils and Incense for Prosperity and Abundance

CEDAR: Protects and enhances your assets
CINNAMON: Encourages financial gain from a successful career or business endeavor
CLOVE: Stimulates financial growth
VERVAIN: Helps your financial goals materialize

Essential Oils and Incense for Protection

ANISE (STAR): Protects against negative energy
FENNEL: Provides physical and psychic protection
PINE: Guards against negativity and evil spirits

Essential Oils and Incense for Health and Healing

EUCALYPTUS: Relieves congestion and soothes colds
LAVENDER: Encourages relaxation and sleep
SWEET MARJORAM: Eases muscle and joint pain/stiffness

Essential Oils and Incense for Personal and Professional Success

CEDAR: Encourages prosperity and protects against adversaries

CINNAMON: Speeds career success and wealth

PATCHOULI: Stimulates enthusiasm and success in any endeavor

SANDALWOOD: Aids mental ability; facilitates guidance and assistance from higher sources

Essential Oils and Incense for Personal and Spiritual Growth

ANISE: Improves psychic vision

BERGAMOT: Elevates mood and increases confidence

LEMON: Clears the mind and makes you more alert

ORANGE: Increases happiness and optimism

Index

NOTE: Page numbers in parentheses indicate intermittent references.

About the Author

SKYE ALEXANDER is the author of more than forty fiction and nonfiction books, many on metaphysical subjects, including five previous titles in the Modern Witchcraft series. She's also an astrologer, tarot reader, feng shui practitioner, and artist. She divides her time between Texas and Massachusetts with her black Manx cat, Zoe. Visit her website, SkyeAlexander.com.

POWERFUL HERBS FOR THE
MODERN-DAY WITCH!

PICK UP OR DOWNLOAD YOUR COPY TODAY!